TAKING GOD TO WORK

the keys to ultimate success

Taking God to Work: *The Keys to Ultimate Success*
© 2018
DAVIWIN Publishing

Printed in the United States of America by DAVIWIN Publishing
First Printing
ISBN 978-0-9977747-9-5

Cover: JD&J Design, LLC
Interior: Gary Jenkins

Contents

Introduction

Section One: God's Plan For Your Work Life

1. Does God Fit In My Briefcase? — 1
2. Beating Temptation at Work — 19
3. What God Thinks About You and Your Work — 45

Section Two: How to Succeed On the Job

4. Finding a Job You Can Love — 59
5. How to Advance In Your Career — 85
6. Pursuing Excellence In a Mediocre World — 105
7. Balancing Life and Work — 123

Section Three: Beating Stress and Discovering Joy At Work

8. Surviving Incompetence and Bad Behavior — 143
9. Living Beyond Paycheck to Paycheck — 163
10. When Your Job Is Driving You Crazy — 183
11. How to Recover From a Big Mistake — 203

Section Four: Winning the Spiritual Endgame

12. Discerning Spiritual Warfare at Work — 223
13. Should Christians Retire? — 245

Epilogue

Praise for TAKING GOD TO WORK

"Steve Reynolds has written a much needed book. For years I've looked for just the perfect book to give to business people in our church, regardless of their faith level. This is that book! I'll be using it as both an individual gift and in our small groups. Highly recommend!"

Nelson Searcy, Founding / Teaching Pastor, The Journey Church NYC and founder, ChurchLeaderInsights.com

"When I see the names on this book I know I can expect excellent writing, a passion to help others change, and inspiration on a timely and timeless topic. This one delivers."

Carole Lewis, First Place 4 Health Director, Emeritus
Author, *Give God A Year* and *Change Your Life Forever*

"Almighty God has given some men the gift to speak into the lives of other men. Steve Reynolds has that gift and his heart is to steward this gift and help build men that would advance the Kingdom of God. We love every opportunity Steve has to speak at an Iron Sharpens Iron Equipping Conference!"

Brian Doyle, Founder and President Iron Sharpens Iron

"Regardless of your age or time in the workforce, this book is an excellent resource aimed at equipping you to share your faith at work. This work by co-authors David Winters and Pastor Steve Reynolds provides valuable biblical work insights from two men that served well in their chosen fields. Weaved within these pages are transparent stories of individuals from a variety of backgrounds in positions that also will inspire you to excellence with character qualities pleasing to God."

Valerie Caraotta, Book Reviewer

Introduction

The co-authors of this book—a pastor of a medium-size church in the Washington, DC, suburbs, and a career-long federal employee and manager—believe strongly in the power of ordinary Christians to transform their jobs, their co-workers, and their employers. This book offers advice and insights on how you can travel the path for lasting success, both in business and in your spiritual walk. Although an unashamedly Christian book, the advice is timeless, and you will find it helpful regardless of where you are on your spiritual journey.

This book features numerous spotlight stories about real people who are taking God to work each day and reaping the rewards of sharing their faith with those around them. The stories include people from all walks of life—from store clerks to leaders of industry and government. Several entrepreneurs also share their secrets for honoring God in their businesses and using His principles to improve the quality of their goods and services. By conquering temptations and traps, real people have found the way to lasting happiness on the job and at home. You can too.

Although you could easily read this book from cover to cover, we have provided study questions and prayers at the end of each chapter, if you wish to go deeper. Substantial portions of the material have been used in a highly successful Christian growth campaign at Capital Baptist Church in Annandale, Virginia, and many of the questions have been tested in Growth Groups to further involve church members. However, as with any study, it will have greater impact if you embrace the ideas and implement the practical how-to suggestions that are offered. All Scripture references come from the New King James Version of the Bible.

When relating anecdotes about the workplace, the co-authors use the terms "I" and "me" to refer to either Pastor Steve Reynolds or David L. Winters. Because Steve has been a pastor all his adult life, and David has worked as a government manager for most of his career, we believe you will easily be able to differentiate the stories told from a manager's experience and those from a pastor's perspective.

We hope this book will help you learn how to maximize your faith at work and grasp hold of lasting success—spiritually, physically, mentally, and financially. Our purpose in writing it was to equip you to make the most of your work life and help create long-term success for you based on biblical principles. We also hope it will help you to gather courage, understand God's tactics, and find your unique mission to bring God's Kingdom to those you meet every day through your job or business.

Applying God's principles to your work will likely lead to many successes and help you overcome challenges as well. The Lord will use your difficulties to build your character and refine your personality to be more like Jesus. To this end, we have devoted much of this book to unpacking the complications of workplace relationships and showing you how to apply biblical wisdom to help you succeed at work. We offer specific strategies to respond to life's challenges, including what to do when you make a major mistake at work, how to handle the feeling you've been forgotten, what to do when you are stabbed in the back by a co-worker, and how to handle sexual temptation when it comes knocking. We will also go into detail in the chapters ahead about how to deal with various stressors.

We believe that with humility and the ideas presented in this book, you will be equipped to share your faith at work while maintaining your professionalism and enhancing your relationships. Your calling is to use your work to care for God's world and the people in it. While no one does this perfectly, most of us wish we could do it better, and this book will show you how to effectively bring God into your workplace.

So, come with us on the journey to recognize these opportunities and make the most of them for eternity.

Steve Reynolds and *David L. Winters*

God's Plan For Your Work Life

DOES GOD FIT IN MY BRIEFCASE?

And whatever you do, do it heartily,
as to the Lord and not to men.
Colossians 3:23

THE DAY STARTED LIKE ANY OTHER on my way to the Department of Homeland Security. After another too-hot summer, the first cool breezes of fall were filling up my Impala as I cruised past Georgetown on the George Washington Parkway. The Christian radio station I was playing laid down peaceful tracks in the background, and I marveled at the beauty of the large trees lining the historic road. Soon my journey to work would take me across the Potomac River and past several of the iconic landmarks of our nation's capital. The Lincoln Memorial, Washington Monument, and the White House stood stoically along Constitution Avenue.

The trip from the outside world to my desk at the Department of Homeland Security included many layers of security. Badges, keycards, chips, frowning guards, and even old-fashioned keys comprised the security measures that had been employed to get me into my small office with a view of the back alley. Once I was seated behind my computer, more chips and passwords stood between me and logging onto the computer system, retrieving emails, and checking out the latest management reports.

Before I had a chance to read the first message, an employee of mine named Martin burst into my office and began ranting about the unreasonable demands of a program manager and his team. "We told them the deadline for the fiscal year was three weeks ago. Last night, they called me into their scientific director's office and demanded that I get this contract out by next week. They don't even have a statement of work!"

I looked over at Martin and tried to calm him with my expression. It had the opposite effect. He became more agitated, because I seemingly had failed to rise to his level of warble. "Martin," I said, "this happens all the time. Have a seat. Let's talk. We either can do it, or we can't. There is no reason to get so upset. Think about your blood pressure."

Not to mention my blood pressure, I said to myself.

Martin sat down, but my gentle rebuke soon triggered a new tirade from him about management being unsupportive and how our mutual boss kept turning up the pressure by over-promising to our customers. At that point, Martin rose from his seat and stood on his chair. He began yelling something perverse as he tried to make me see his level of hysteria.

I quickly lifted up a silent prayer. God gave me some defusing words, and Martin climbed back down from his chair. That's when things got *really* interesting.

"Martin," I said, "you have to look at the big picture here. We are only on this planet for a relatively short time. There is no reason to get this upset. Think about our higher purpose."

"Don't give me that God stuff!" he snapped. "Never talk to me about that again!"

He stomped away from my office, leaving me feeling shaken and alone. Although I had barely alluded to a "higher purpose," he had clearly taken offense. Would he file an Equal Employment Opportunity complaint or just hold a continuously simmering resentment toward me? All I knew at that point was that God needed to be a much bigger part of my daily life at the office. Challenges like this exceeded the shallow faith I had brought along to my work life. While solid in my belief in Christ, perhaps I had separated faith from my work.

Why and How Do You Take God to Work?

Obviously, the first step to taking God anywhere is to ask Him into your life—not just to be your Savior, but also your LORD. The Bible is the story of His love for mankind, and you in particular. If you are not yet a believer, please do come along. I'm praying that by the end of this book, you would like to join millions of others who take God to work each day.

God never intended you to function in this world on a solo basis. He wants to be actively engaged in all parts of your life. Believers have the Holy Spirit as a resident within them, but God wants to be your President. He wants to tear down the wall of partition between your work life and your spiritual life. Not only can you consult with Him at work, but you can also co-labor with Him. If you accept His challenge, He will help you to be your best and make the most of every opportunity. Will you take the challenge to influence your workplace in a positive way for Christ?

If you already believe in Jesus as your LORD and Savior, the next step is to make the leap from believer to follower. It takes a leap of faith to believe in God, but it takes a leap of the will to become a disciple of Jesus. At a time in history when forces are shouting at believers to sit down, will you have the courage and skills to practice your faith on the job? Will you follow Jesus to the very end of your career—let alone your life?

God Created Work Before the Fall

Like every life-giving thing, God created work. In Genesis 2:5, we read that there existed "no man to till the ground." So, God created men and women to work in the Garden and take care of the world. God wants to have fellowship with mankind as we enjoy and use all aspects of His creation, including work. From the earliest times until now, the primary purpose of work has been for men and women to take care of God's world and each other. Whether our current role is to clean hotel rooms or manage a Fortune 500 company, our efforts care for our fellow travelers here.

Work is fundamentally a good thing. It brings purpose to our lives. It brings structure to meeting our basic and most complex needs. God introduced work before mankind first disobeyed Him (which is known as the Fall of mankind.) God's intention has always been that we will find something worthwhile to do with our energy, brain power, and love for others. When we combine our vocation with our spiritual mission, it produces supernatural dynamite that moves mountains and clears the way for great accomplishments.

Work is also good for us mentally and physically. Sadly, in life we lose those things we don't use, exercise, or develop. Our unused talent atrophies and sometimes leaves us forever. Working is human-life exercise that builds character, defines our motives, and teaches us valuable lessons.

If we accept the premise that work is intrinsically good, then as Christians our labors should be specially blessed. In Colossians 3:23, Paul directs us to do our work with dedication, as if we work for the LORD directly instead of merely working for a human boss. If you ever lack motivation, think about the King of the Universe looking on as you do your job. He notices when you review that important document for the second time to ensure the quality, even if your earthly boss won't notice. The LORD knows, and He will reward you accordingly somewhere down the road—if not on earth, then in heaven.

Working as unto the LORD has a potentially world-changing side effect. Your co-workers may see your extra effort and realize there is something different about you. Jesus said, "Let your light so shine before men, that they may see your good works and glorify your Father in heaven" (Matthew 5:16). Enthusiasm, a good attitude, and even exhibiting joy in spite of tough times will draw attention to you in a good way. Working unto God doesn't mean you have the license to ignore your earthly boss, but this principle will instill an extra motivator to keep you working diligently when no one is looking.

Your Boss Is a Gift from God

While you may think your boss came straight from the pit of hell, he or she actually became an authority in the world with God's approval. Isn't that a mind-blowing thought? With all of your boss's idiosyncrasies, character flaws, and physical imperfections, God has approved him or her (at least tacitly) to be in your life for this season. Although the passage of Scripture that supports this idea deals specifically with governmental leaders, the same principle is true about the authorities at your work:

> Let every soul be subject to the governing authorities. For there is no authority except from God, and the authorities that exist are appointed by God. Therefore whoever resists the authority resists the ordinance of God, and those who resist will bring judgment on themselves. For rulers are not a terror to good works, but to evil. Do you want to be unafraid of the authority? Do what is good, and you will have praise from the same. For he is God's minister to you for good (Romans 13:1–4).

What an amazing idea. Your leader, supervisor, or foreman acts on God's behalf during the time he or she is your boss to bring order to your world. As you try to do good things and accomplish the mission of your company or organization, your boss will be a blessing to you. If you do good things and contribute to success in the workplace, you will earn praise that is sent from

God. Your boss can become a minister to you for good to keep you on the right track.

The challenge is that if you resist your boss's authority, you could well be resisting God's authority over your life. Opposing or trying to circumvent authority at work is actually the opposite of accepting God's will. The penalties of opposing your boss's authority is further explained in the next few verses of this passage in Romans:

> But if you do evil, be afraid; for he does not bear the sword in vain; for he is God's minister, an avenger to execute wrath on him who practices evil. Therefore you must be subject, not only because of wrath but also for conscience' sake. For because of this you also pay taxes, for they are God's ministers attending continually to this very thing. Render therefore to all their due: taxes to whom taxes are due, customs to whom customs, fear to whom fear, honor to whom honor (Romans 13:4–7).

The secret is to look beyond your earthly boss and see the Father as your employer. Think of God as the Chief Executive Officer (CEO) of all employers. He wants you to follow the instructions of your day-to-day manager, but He is above that person on the organization chart. He is your friend and always available, with His office door open. You can come to God at any time and talk over all situations with Him. No appointment is needed.

This principle has played out many times during the course of my thirty-three-year work life. When I represented my earthly leaders well and worked hard for their agenda, amazing blessings flowed my way. Promotions, bonuses, and awards piled up as I worked as unto God for my bosses. Conversely, when I got on the wrong side of my boss, everything seemed out of whack. I'm not talking about short-term disagreements over the right path ahead, but times when my attitude became less than supportive of my management. When this happened, something had to give. Thankfully, each time God helped me transition to a different job relatively quickly, or He moved the leader onto his or her next challenge. Either way, I learned a lesson about authority from each of these encounters.

No doubt, someone out there is thinking about Hitler or another evil boss. Did God allow Hitler to be someone's boss? The answer is yes, even Hitler. "The LORD has made all for Himself, yes, even the wicked for the day of doom" (Proverbs 16:4). Remember that Paul penned Romans 13 when the Roman Emperor Nero ruled. Even with this despot on the throne, Paul charged believers to respect the ruling authorities. There are times when you may find yourself with terrible, evil supervisors. In those cases, God may use you to respectfully speak into their lives. You can pray for them and do your best to influence them for good. But if they don't turn around, God is able to transition you away from bad leaders. God did it for me multiple times.

Life and Work Are Difficult

Although our boss is a gift from God and work is a good thing, it became difficult after sin entered the picture. In Genesis 3:17–19, we read how God cursed the ground:

> Cursed is the ground for your sake; in toil you shall eat of it all the days of your life. Both thorns and thistles it shall bring forth for you, and you shall eat the herb of the field. In the sweat of your face you shall eat bread till you return to the ground, for out of it you were taken; for dust you are, and to dust you shall return.

Understanding that work can, at times, be difficult and challenging should have the positive effect of changing our expectations. If we presume that being redeemed will make every moment of our work lives easy, we are sorely mistaken. "Man who is born of woman is of few days and full of trouble" (Job 14:1). There will be trouble in this fallen world. We, as Christians, will experience our share, but Jesus will see us through the storms if we build our foundation on Him. Without this understanding, each problem or obstacle will seem exaggerated in size and scope. We need to recognize that work includes difficult challenges and be prepared to tackle each problem as a hill to climb over, not a brick wall to halt our progress.

The good news of the gospel includes God's comfort. He promises to bring relief to our souls when we are troubled. Just look, for example, at how Paul was comforted:

> I am filled with comfort. I am exceedingly joyful in all our tribulation. For indeed, when we came to Macedonia, our bodies had no rest, but we were troubled on every side. Outside were conflicts, inside were fears. Nevertheless God, who comforts the downcast, comforted us (2 Corinthians 7:4–6).

God wants to comfort us as well with peace inside.

With our redemption, bought by Christ on the cross, we will experience the blessing of God's help, but it will not necessarily make our labor easy or without effort. However, we have a friend "who sticks closer than a brother" (Proverbs 18:24), helping us navigate the waters of our workplace. So, how does God help us at work? His Word teaches us principles that lead to success. He often answers our specific prayers to overcome obstacles, bless specific meetings or projects, apply wisdom to difficult problems, and give us joy in hard times. As we walk in God's promises and obey His commands, our work will bear fruit, and we will be blessed. God promises to direct our paths and show favor to His children.

The Secret to Getting Paid

God's plan for work remains solid today. If we work at something that is valued by people, either individually or collectively, we get paid. If that work is valuable to God, we will also get a spiritual reward in heaven. Any legitimate work that involves caring for people and doesn't involve sin is part of God's plan to care for the world. The key for us as Christians is to connect our earthly work to God's value system.

God's eternal plan for work is that our productive efforts will take care of His world. He uses our nine-to-five jobs or our businesses to feed, clothe, house, warm, and provide for His creation. When we partner with God in this exercise, He makes our work easier, more productive, and more satisfying. The Holy Spirit leads us to the truly valuable experiences of life. Beyond our direct efforts to care for others through our work, earning a paycheck enables us to support God's work locally and all around the world. What an incredible opportunity! Paying tithes and giving offerings multiplies our effectiveness beyond the physical touch of our direct efforts to people throughout our community and around the globe.

Heavenly Repayment

As you've added eternal value at your workplace, a reward has been accruing for you in heaven. This eternal currency is different from earthly money, because it doesn't rust, doesn't suffer the effects of inflation, and it won't get stolen. Whether you work in an office, retail establishment, or at home, you will likely get the amazing opportunity to come into contact with others through in-person exchanges, phone calls, emails, or other communications.

God is a worker, and He created us in His image. As Paul wrote, "For by Him all things were created that are in heaven and that are on earth, visible and invisible, whether thrones or dominions or principalities or powers. All things were created through Him and for Him. And He is before all things, and in Him all things consist" (Colossians 1:16–17).

Jesus worked throughout His adult life, first as a carpenter and later as a minister. God meant for us to be workers, whether we work at a job, by volunteering, or at home in the family. God judges our work and will reward us based on our efforts. This isn't to say our salvation is determined by our works—that is by faith alone—but we have the promise that if we work diligently, "knowing that whatever good anyone does, he will receive the same from the LORD" (Ephesians 6:8). When we decide to work for God at our workplace, He becomes our employer.

Given that work is good and believers will be rewarded for their diligence, it might sound like smooth sailing for us. If only that were the case. For those of us who have actually worked at a job, we know that dangers, toils, and snares lurk around many corners of the office or other work environment. Relationships with people can get very complicated.

God's Love at Work

One of the most powerful tools in the Christian's toolbox is love. When we take love with us to work, more than any other trait, it will set us apart. Loving or demonstrating acts of kindness toward our co-workers, supervisors, and customers is a major opportunity and a rich benefit of work. Christians are to "love one another, for love is of God; and everyone who loves is born of God and knows God. He who does not love does not know God, for God is love" (1 John 4:7–8).

Even in the midst of the death, decay, and discouragement of today's world, love shines outward. Love cannot be faked for very long. If we exhibit *agape* love—self-sacrificing love—on the job, people will feel it. Love is the light that shines from the Christian soul walking in the Spirit. Because work is already a way of taking care of people, love is a natural motivator to keep us performing when our patience, energy, or selfish motives run out.

Rest

In a high-pressure environment, the stress battle sometimes begins during the commute to work. Angry drivers, unruly subway passengers, or day-dreaming homeless people may stress our frayed nerves. Then we arrive at the office or job site, just in time to beat the clock and figure out what's on our plate for the new day. A mountain of unread emails greets us and gives us the uncomfortable feeling we are already behind. But God has an answer to all these pressures. If we are in need of intensive care for stress, we can take this gentle advice as a start: *do your best work each day, and then give it a rest.*

As we've already discussed, God instituted a system of work, but He also created a system of regular rest. In Genesis 2, we read how God rested from His labors. After six days of work creating the universe, He took a day off. We should do the same. The ability to continue walking in love is dependent on our ability to renew and refresh ourselves along the way. Days off and vacations give us the replenishment we need to meet the challenges ahead. Daily times of prayer and Bible study, like a mini-retreat, fill us up spiritually. Prayer gives us the renewal to keep the right attitude at our workplace and at home. We need these times of refreshing from the LORD to handle all the responsibilities of our modem world.

Resting has many purposes, but three are particularly important. First, *rest refocuses our spirit.* Our eternal spirit can be drawn this way and that by our circumstances and the people around us. Resting, particularly with worship, allows us to refocus on God. "And [God] said to them, 'The Sabbath was made for man, and not man for the Sabbath'" (Mark 2:27). God knew we needed to rest and reset at regular intervals. He programmed in the whole waking and sleep cycle. We sleep every night and are resurrected each morning. It is all part of our body's resetting process and a picture of God's ability to eventually resurrect us from death.

Second, *rest recharges our emotions.* Life would be really boring without emotions. Highs and lows are normal. Love, hate, joy, and sadness are just some of the many emotions that are part of the game of life. Sometimes, we can overdose on emotions. We need to settle down and calm down at regular intervals. In 1 Thessalonians 5:11, Paul encouraged the believers to pause for the refreshment of fellowship: "Therefore comfort each other and edify one another, just as you also are doing."

Third, *rest replenishes our bodies.* Aside from all its other functions, rest allows our body to heal itself. Every system in our body benefits from the sleep cycle. Exercise and moving around is important, but exercise only benefits us if it is followed by rest. "And [Jesus] said to them, 'Come aside by yourselves to a deserted place and rest a while.' For there were many coming and going, and they did not even have time to eat" (Mark 6:31).

Taking God to a Fallen World of Work

The workplace, like all facets of our fallen world, is a battlefield between good and evil. Christians must be wise about the environment in which they find themselves.

For the past forty years, a seismic shift has been occurring in attitudes about morality. It began during the turmoil of the 1970s and grew, slowly at first, into a movement that no longer supports biblical principles about sexuality, marriage, authority, or even the importance of human life. Whereas forty years ago most people and employers promoted marriage, current attitudes lean more toward an "anything goes" morality—if it is consensual and everyone is happy, let the good times roll. In government, as in most companies, progressive forces have pushed the envelope in an attempt to win society's approval of their morality.

In addition to not supporting biblical values, many workplaces now prohibit Christians from saying even a word of opposition about non-biblical relationships or living arrangements. *Sin* is not a term that is welcome in most workplaces, and Christians often wonder how far the pendulum will eventually swing. Is there ever going to be a point when godliness will again be valued at work? Furthermore, how can Christians live out their faith without fear of reprisal? We know that following God's principles produces a happier life than ignoring His scriptural warnings, but we may be hesitant to tell our co-workers about the benefits out of fear.

At times, it seems as if it is open season on Christians. Evil schemes are at work to keep us quiet and promote spiritual decay across the globe. If we do speak out about Jesus in the workplace, the consequences could result in anything from mild ostracizing by co-workers to formal disciplinary action from supervisory managers. As a result, many of us have retreated into a shell. We avoid conflict at almost any cost—in spite of the biblical admonition to "sanctify the LORD God in your hearts, and always be ready to give a defense to everyone who asks you a reason for the hope that is in you, with meekness and fear" (1 Peter 3:15).

Did you hear the last part of that verse? It provides a major clue about how we can share our faith without ruffling feathers unnecessarily. Humility, while it sometimes seems a rarely practiced discipline, opens doors. Timing and self-awareness are the keys.

Summary

God created work before the Fall of mankind and intended work for our good. His purposes for our work include taking care of His creation and using our unique gifts to meet the needs of others. By connecting our earthly job to God's purposes, we can please God and earn rewards in heaven. God's system of work includes a plan for rest, which recharges us and makes us more effective for future work. Though work is essentially good, it can be difficult in our fallen world.

Spotlight Feature

Jonathan Tack

Jonathan Tack, a chief pilot for a small aircraft services firm, considers his current position his "dream job." His firm began when a few of his friends decided to create a business that would be run on Christian values. Working with friends who are also respected colleagues has yielded several advantages in his life.

"This is definitely the best job I've ever had," Jonathan says. "I know everyone who works here and respect them. This Midland, Texas, company is committed to godly values and to missions." A Christian, for-profit company, the employees and owners meet together and draft goals for missions giving, which come out of the company's profits. In 2017, they met their giving goals by July. Beyond just donating money, they are working with authorities in a central African country, trying to leverage their business relationship with a pre-positioned mission organization there. If it all works out, the officials at Jonathan's company intend to

bring general aviation into new places as an economic opportunity and conduit for the gospel.

"The whole culture of the company is Christian," Jonathan
says. "We are committed to showing excellence in every regard
as a witness to those we serve." Employees conduct themselves
and live in a way that reflects Christ's love to their customers.

For Jonathan, a typical day involves first going to the plane
he will be flying for that day. Sometimes, this is locally in Fort
Worth, but at other times it is a plane parked in another city.
The planes that Jonathan flies are owned by other companies
or private individuals who need a pilot for a single flight or a
longer trip. Jonathan's employer ensures required flight plans
are filed and maintenance and/or warranty logs are updated. As
the pilot, Jonathan then flies the plane to the chosen destination.
Depending on the length of time the client will be in the other
city, Jonathan will either stay in that city or return to Midland.

According to Jonathan, faith has been a big part of getting
their company off the ground. God helps them each day in
response to their prayers. He has sent customers at the right
times and in the right quantities to keep the company from
being overwhelmed or over-extended. Going forward, they
plan to continue depending on God as they grow and expand.

Although working as a pilot in a Christian environment
is Jonathan's dream job, he admits God uses challenges and
dilemmas there to help him grow. Benefits so far have included
developing patience, proving God's faithfulness, and testing the
limits of his integrity. Jonathan also finds that he spends more
time praying and interceding. His plans include humbly confess-
ing God's sovereignty and trusting Him to bring the company
more business so they can expand their mission's contributions
around the world.

Jonathan recently attended a Christian businessmen's conference and resonated with the speaker's message that the gospel
has always been spread by business people. Original missionaries

had jobs. Church planters took the gospel with them on their business travels. They brought seeds of faith along with their spices, textiles, and other products. Just as Jonathan's company has high ideals, he seeks to pursue excellence every day. "I want to demonstrate an unusual loyalty and commitment to customer service," he says, "along with a strong work ethic."

Over the years, Jonathan has learned it is not smart to have separation between his work persona and his Christian persona. He encourages others to be stellar colleagues and businesspeople—to make themselves valuable and do the best they can, for getting recognized as a child of Christ depends on it. To Jonathan, being excellent is a major way to stay relevant to the culture and those he serves.

Spotlight Questions

What could you identify with in Jonathan's story?

What action steps occurred to you about taking God to work?

Study Questions

1   *Read Colossians 3:23 and Romans 13:1.* Paul encourages believers to do their jobs as unto the Lord. Do you know a person who lives (or lived) up to this admonition?

2   What resulted from that believer's commitment to serve God through his or her work? How did it effect that person's life and the lives of his or her co-workers?

3   How does knowing that God has set authorities in your life change your attitude toward your earthly bosses and leaders?

4   What are the advantages of praying for your supervisor or leader?

5   *Read Colossians 1:16–17.* We know that God created the world and everything in it. What impact should this knowledge have on your work?

6   The Bible says we have been created by God and for God. How should this set you apart in your work?

7   Do you have any personal experiences regarding sharing faith in the workplace? How did you share it? How was it received—positively or negatively?

8   *Read Mark 2:27 and 6:31.* Why do you think God emphasizes rest after working?

9   How do you relax on the weekends after a hard week at work?

10   Read 1 Peter 3:15. When was a time you took this advice and shared the hope in your heart with a co-worker?

11   Peter admonishes us to "always be ready to give testimony." How can you make sure you are ready to do this?

12   What do you hope to get out of reading this book and/or discussing it with others?

Prayer

Lord, as You resurrect me each morning this week, teach me how to fulfill my purpose of caring for the world. Please accept my praise and offerings for the new day. Multiply Your love to my supervisors, co-workers, and clients/customers. Teach me about Your loving kindness and how You care for me each day of the week. Grant me satisfaction with the results of my labor and my salary earned. Grant me and my family safety and peace as we travel to and from work. As I thankfully end each day, enable me to sleep well each night, knowing that You are faithful to fill in for those tasks that I missed or didn't get done. Finally, please grant me and my co-laborers joy for our journey, a smile for each stranger, and contentment in abundant measure. In the name of Jesus, Amen.

What will you do to take God to work this week?

BEATING TEMPTATION
AT WORK

There is no fear in love; but perfect love casts out fear, because fear involves torment. But he who fears has not been made perfect in love.
1 John 4:18

As SENIOR PASTOR of Capital Baptist Church in Annandale, Virginia, I minister to an eclectic congregation representing dozens of countries and almost every work background common to the region. The members occupy jobs at every station of life, from high-ranking government officials to cashiers at the local fast food restaurant. Located just outside Washington, DC, the church is a medium-size congregation, with about 800 in attendance on Sunday mornings. In anticipation of writing this book, I asked this congregation, "What is your number one temptation at work?" Including Facebook comments, I received more than 200 responses to that question.

The following represent the dirty dozen work temptations in reverse order.

Top Twelve Temptations at Work

12. FEAR

Human beings are prone to fear. In fact, it is perhaps one of the major drivers that energizes the world of business. Whether it is fear we will lose our job or fear the company will cease to exist, it motivates so much of what happens within the four walls of an office. Government organizations are far from exempt. Without the profit motive, they thrive on survival instincts. *Take no chances. Don't get into trouble. Avoid anything remotely risky.*

Heaven's economy is the opposite of our earthly fear-based ones. It is faith-based. Jesus put it this way: "Now if God so clothes the grass of the field, which today is, and tomorrow is thrown into the oven, will He not much more clothe you, O you of little faith?" (Matthew 6:30). If we want to follow Jesus at work, we have to conquer our fears. Sure, this is easier said than done, but it is not impossible with God.

The key to avoiding a fear mentality is love. "There is no fear in love; but perfect love casts out fear, because fear involves torment. But he who fears has not been made perfect in love" (1 John 4:18). We have to think about, meditate on, and immerse ourselves in God's love for us. The Creator of the whole universe loves *you*. He is always thinking about you, your life, your problems, and your workplace.

Could any thought be more awesome? No matter where you go or what you do, God is watching over you. He loves you. In the end, you will not be defeated as long as you trust in the LORD.

11. COMPROMISING BELIEFS

Biblical standards are much higher than the standards held by most people and companies, and Christians can feel pressured at times to compromise their beliefs. However, we have to remember that God keeps His covenant with us and His love will constrain us, if we allow it to do so. Remembering all that God has done and continues to do for us will make it difficult, if not impossible, for us to compromise our faith. "Therefore know that the LORD your God, He is God, the faithful God who keeps covenant and mercy for a thousand generations with those who love Him and keep His commandments" (Deuteronomy 7:9).

10. STEALING FROM THE COMPANY

Although it may sound surprising, many Christians are tempted to steal from their company in both small and large ways. Whether it is pilfering pens or stealing time by surfing the Internet instead of working, all stealing is wrong. We are paid to do our job. "Let him who stole steal no longer, but rather let him labor, working with his hands what is good, that he may have something to give him who has need" (Ephesians 4:28).

9. LYING

Lying is a dangerous game, because before long it can become a habit. Eventually, if we keep on lying, our conscience becomes seared to the point we can no longer be honest even with ourselves. Some have bought into the lie that their job requires "fudging the truth" at times, but the reality is that lying is part of our "old man" behavior. "Do not lie to one another, since you have put off the old man with his deeds" (Colossians 3:9).

8. OVEREATING OR EATING UNHEALTHY FOODS

One of the most nurturing acts a human can perform is to provide food to another person. It speaks life and encouragement to the soul on a deep level. Unfortunately, symbolic confusion results when the food provided is grossly unhealthy. We find this in many offices today, where traditions include serving unhealthy foods from donuts to rich desserts at certain functions.

For Christians who are trying to become or stay healthy, this can be a temptation. "Do you not know that your body is the temple of the Holy Spirit who is in you, whom you have from

God, and you are not your own? For you were bought at a price; therefore glorify God in your body and in your spirit, which are God's" (1 Corinthians 6:19–20). When it is our turn to bring food into the office, we can turn around some of these unhealthy traditions. We can be creative and thoughtful in making an effort to bring food and beverages that are healthy *and* taste good. When others bring in highly caloric or unhealthy treats, we can set an example by thanking them for their thoughtfulness while abstaining. Usually, one or two sentences about "watching our weight" is all that is needed. Before long, they won't even ask us to engage in eating the unhealthy foods they have brought into the office.

7. COMPLAINING

Everyone has likes and dislikes. At work, certain tasks invoke great pleasure while others are arduous. One way to quickly set ourselves apart is to avoid complaining. While it is fine to scope out a new project and explain the obstacles that have to be overcome, it is important to immediately follow this up with a *solution*. Generally, everyone can see the negatives—we don't have to be the first to point them out. So, if you do find it necessary to bring up a problem, be sure to focus on the fix or solution. Otherwise, you will soon be labeled as the office complainer. "Do all things without complaining and disputing" (Philippians 2:14).

6. ANGER

Anger in and of itself is not always wrong. A word study of the Old or New Testament yields examples of God becoming angry with various kinds of bad behaviors. Paul, under the inspiration of the Holy Spirit, wrote, "'Be angry, and do not sin:' do not let the sun go down on your wrath" (Ephesians 4:26). This verse speaks of righteous anger, which includes expressing anger at sin and its consequences. Yet even then, we are told to express anger only in a controlled manner (see James 1:19–20).

Often, we will be tempted to express unrighteous anger when we feel our personal rights have been violated. We then strike back in anger as an act of vengeance, which is sin (see Romans 12:19–21). In business, however, getting angry—regardless of whether it is righteous or unrighteous—is almost always the wrong move. When we lose control of our emotions, we seldom win arguments or friends.

If you feel anger starting to rise up at work, call on the Holy Spirit to bring peace into the situation. "An angry man stirs up strife, and a furious man abounds in transgression" (Proverbs 29:22). Believers should never be the ones stirring the pot or making trouble over minor issues. Rather, they should be peacemakers whenever possible.

5. LAZINESS

Everyone has an off day now and then. People are not machines—and who among us has not been distracted by problems with a loved one or a car in need of repair? Laziness, however, is a regular pattern of just doing the minimum. It can cause many problems for a company or organization, because productivity is the key to profits and success.

Planes have fallen from the sky because someone didn't keep up with the required maintenance. Car brakes have failed because an auto worker decided to goof off on a Friday afternoon. "He who is slothful in his work is a brother to him who is a great destroyer" (Proverbs 18:9). When you remember that your work is God's hand extended to take care of the world, it becomes much easier to stay motivated. "Not lagging in diligence, fervent in spirit, serving the LORD" (Romans 12:11).

4. CURSING/SWEARING

As Christians, our witness may be the only example of Jesus that some people see on a regular basis. We don't want to be an excuse for anyone not to believe. Using foul language is never necessary, and often it is just a bad habit. If this is a problem for you, team up with the Holy Spirit and obey His voice when He reminds you to clean up your speech. "Let no corrupt word proceed out of your mouth, but what is good for necessary edification, that it may impart grace to the hearers" (Ephesians 4:29).

3. MISUSING TECHNOLOGY

One would have to be living under a rock to not notice that technology has dramatically changed during the past thirty years, and it will continue to rapidly evolve the way we work and the tasks we perform. Technology can open up incredible possibilities for Christians to be salt and light at their workplace. However, like most tools, it can also be used for evil, for with great opportunities come great temptations. Almost daily, one hears of another scandal about a public figure who misused technology at work or among co-workers. Many times, these indiscretions lead to firing, disgrace, or worse.

Although most employees today know enough to not use work computers for pornography, many still spend too much time browsing the Internet. There is a plethora of ways to misuse technology, but almost all of them involve wasting time. (See "laziness" above.) We are paid for a full day's work, and we should be focusing on work, regardless of the location.

Christians have a great opportunity to shine the light of Christ and be an example at our jobs. As in every other aspect of life, someone is watching us. Our greatest power as Christian employees is our motivation to work as unto the LORD regardless of whether other people see our efforts or don't see them. This witness is stronger than any words we could speak. For example, many businesses and government offices encourage employees to work from home, which can test our self-discipline and diligence on a daily basis. Does our productivity go up when we work from home? Are we watching game shows on television when we are supposed to be creating a presentation? Or does our efficiency increase because we are not having to deal with all the interruptions that define our office life?

2. GOSSIPING

Conversations can quickly turn to gossip if they have negative connotations and the person being discussed isn't there to defend himself or herself. The most outlandish rumors are exchanged by those who have trained their minds to enjoy spreading gossip. "And besides they learn to be idle, wandering about from house to house, and not only idle but also gossips and busybodies, saying things which they ought not" (1 Timothy 5:13). The best way to avoid gossip is to avoid those who spread it. If that isn't an option, a quick word about checking with the subject of the rumor is usually enough to shut down inappropriate talk (at least in your presence). "A perverse man sows strife, and a whisperer separates the best of friends" (Proverbs 16:28).

1. SEXUAL MISCONDUCT/ROMANCE

Office romances have sunk many careers. While they seldom last, employees may spend years feeling awkward around the former object of their affection. For the Christian, engaging in sexual activity with another outside of marriage is sin and can have the unintended consequence of badly damaging our witness to non-believers. It also negatively impacts our relationship with God. Some sources suggest as high as seventy percent of all adulterous affairs begin at work. Many marriages have failed because one partner or another became involved with a co-worker. "Therefore put to death your members which are on the earth: fornication, uncleanness, passion, evil desire, and covetousness, which is idolatry" (Colossians 3:5).

One of the most famous stories about sexual temptation in the Bible involves the patriarch Joseph and his boss's wife. As told in Genesis 39:1–12, Joseph experienced God's favor and became successful in Egypt. An officer of Pharaoh named Potiphar trusted Joseph and made him overseer of his house. Under Joseph's care, the whole house prospered, and everything went well at first. But in this environment of success, temptation soon reared its ugly head. Potiphar's wife became attracted to Joseph, because she found him "handsome in form and appearance." She looked at him with longing and said, "Lie with me" (verses 6–7).

Joseph maintained his integrity, cited his loyalty to Potiphar, and pleaded with her not to pursue him in this way. Finally, he said, "There is no one greater in this house than I, nor has he kept back anything from me but you, because you are his wife. How then can I do this great wickedness, and sin against God?" (verse 9). None of this slowed her down. Day after day, she kept after him. Finally, she grabbed him by his garment, and he had to run away without it to escape her intentions. Sometimes, you have to do the same thing. Is a job more important than your marriage? Is flirting with a co-worker more important than your reputation?

All sin begins as an inside problem. "For from within, out of the heart of men, proceed evil thoughts, adulteries, fornications, murders, thefts, covetousness, wickedness, deceit, lewdness, an evil eye, blasphemy, pride, foolishness" (Mark 7:21–22). The origin also leads to the cure. Changes must happen in your inner being. When you lack the capability to make those changes on your own, God is there is to help.

Three Remedies to Help You Resist Temptation

Whether it is in the secretary's office of a cabinet-level governmental department or a Verizon call center, employees can see their workplace as either a well-defined mission field or an intimidating minefield. Overwhelmingly, my church members expressed a desire to overcome temptations and model Christ to their co-workers. So, what are some ways to resist these temptations that often stand in the way of us doing this?

- *Remember the presence of God is always there for you.* As a believer, God promised never to leave you or forsake you (see Hebrews 13:5). His Holy Spirit wants to lead you into all truth and be the answer to your temptation. Pray and ask for that wisdom.

- *Recognize the larger plan that only God fully knows and controls.* Ask how you can help Him accomplish His purposes for your company or organization. God will show you the next right thing to do.
- *Rely on God's power to fight spiritual battles.* "I will lift up my eyes to the hills—from whence comes my help? My help comes from the LORD, who made heaven and earth" (Psalm 121:1–2). God will fight any spiritual forces that are unseen to you. With one word, He can change an entire situation. He wants to do that for you, right where you work.

Over the years, I have heard it all—from members who gave in to sexual sin at work to church guests who felt too ashamed of their sinful past to join Christian fellowship. Yet we need to remember the gospel message brings hope. We can repent of past transgressions and find new mercy in the light of the cross. God has compassion for us, regardless of the extent of our sinful past.

Opportunity in Diversity

American society is becoming ever more inclusive of people of every race and ethnic background. Capital Baptist Church looks a lot like the U.S., with people of many races, ethnicities, and backgrounds represented. God loves all of His creation, in its entirety and with its diversity, and Christians are called to do the same. Differences of language, thought, and culture can make our institutions stronger by inviting innovation, offering new ideas, and compelling employees to share new learning methods or styles.

Diversity has many advantages, and Christians should be at the forefront of promoting them. We have nothing to fear in learning about other cultures, because we already know the right spiritual path, the real Creator of the universe, and His guidebook, the Bible. We know there is no other way to the Father except through His Son, Jesus Christ. "I am the way, the truth and the life. No one comes to the Father except through Me" (John 14:6).

As long as we stay in God's Word and continue in fellowship with Bible-believing Christians, we can remain confident about staying on track spiritually. As Jesus taught, "I am the vine, you are the branches. He who abides in Me, and I in him, bears much fruit; for without Me you can do nothing" (John 15:5). That connected posture gives us our strength, our joy, and the right attitudes at work.

Ideas Come in Three Flavors

Of course, diversity of race and ethnicity is different from diversity of thought. All people are equally important in God's sight, but not all ideologies are equally valid. Some thoughts are not from God, and some ideas can lead many people astray from the truth and the right path.

Ideas come in three categories: (1) they are neutral, (2) they oppose the truth, or (3) they line up with the truth. An example of something in the *neutral* category is that you may prefer red while another person prefers green. Both are fine colors, and neither position is right or wrong. Ideas can be like colors, neutral to the truth.

However, some ideas *oppose the truth*, or are patently false. For example, you may have the idea to jump from the roof of your three-story house because you believe you will not be harmed. This assertion is likely to be proven wrong when you jump onto the sidewalk below.

Other ideas *line up with the truth*. These ideas are true and may be demonstrated as such. For example, if you subject pure water to temperatures below thirty-two degrees Fahrenheit for a long enough time, the water will freeze and solidify. This is a constant law of nature, and it can be proven to be true.

Discerning Truth

There is also a difference between *natural* truth and *spiritual* truth. For the Christian, spiritual truth is proclaimed in the Bible. "All Scripture is given by inspiration of God, and is profitable for doctrine, for reproof, for correction, for instruction in righteousness" (2 Timothy 3:16). Ideas that oppose God's Word are therefore not true. Societies will, for periods of time, wholly attest to spiritual falsehoods. A good example of this is that for a period of time in the past, many people believed the earth was flat. Conventional wisdom indicated that sailing too far west would lead a boat to the edge of the world and put it in danger of falling off.

In the name of progress and diversity, some governments, businesses, secular organizations, and even churches have marched toward accepting various spiritually false ideas. During the last thirty to forty years, immorality in sexual relationships, confusion about gender identity, and disrespect for human life have been institutionalized into laws, regulations, and corporate policies. While the heart behind some of these changes appears to be good, the reality is that sin eventually ends in death. Sin damages the soul and pollutes the mind.

In an attempt to end legitimate evils, like bullying and discrimination, the powers that be may select cures that are worse than the disease. Some of these philosophies of men are backing Christians into a corner by compelling them to accept and even promote sin. Christians have choices about how to respond. Remember the famous quote from Edmund Burke: "The only thing necessary for the triumph of evil is for good men to do nothing."

Temptations When Facing False Ideas

When we are confronted with evil ideas, we may be tempted to remain quiet and do nothing. It is often easier to get along by going along—and we have scriptural instruction to respect the authority of those over us in our jobs and in government. But what should we do when authorities choose an evil path? The first thing we must do is remember that we are not warring against people. "For we do not wrestle against flesh and blood,

but against principalities, against powers, against the rulers of
the darkness of this age, against spiritual hosts of wickedness
in the heavenly places" (Ephesians 6:12).

Once we get that perspective, it should bring us to our knees
in prayer. There is no way to win a spiritual war exclusively in
the flesh. Our calling is to bring God's light, His Word, and
His power into the conflict by praying Jesus into every situation.
We don't act recklessly but bring the matter to the Lord and
ask Him what we can say or do that might delay or prevent
ungodly ideas from being institutionalized.

Another temptation we might face when confronted with
false ideas is to fight against those who are championing the
immoral causes. However, this kind of personal animosity will
only lead down an unproductive path and hinder our mission
to lead our enemies to Christ. As Paul noted in the passage
above, it isn't primarily *people* who we are fighting against. We
love people, notice their amazing qualities and God-created
humanity, care about them personally, and pray for them. But
we also need to oppose, with the shrewdness of a snake, their
wicked schemes. We can't concentrate on the personalities but,
in prayer, on the evil scheme.

The final temptation we might face is to get confused about
compassion. Some followers of Christ believe the best way to
love people is to accept their sin and help them continue in
it. God knows this strategy doesn't work for believers—or we
would not have repented from our sin—and sinful living won't
work for others either. The only way to deal with sin is to label
it, repent of it, and accept God's free gift of forgiveness. Other
people's sin should not be the number one thing on our minds,
but we have to be careful not to let their wrong choices become
a stumbling block for us. In other words, we have to maintain
a sharp edge in recognizing sin compared to purity and God's
standard.

What Can We Do About Company Policies?

As Christians, we do not control all policies, rules, and decisions of our superiors. However, as long as we willingly choose to work within the infrastructure of our employer, it is our obligation not to discriminate, ostracize, or otherwise try to harm people whom we feel are not living up to biblical standards. This doesn't mean we necessarily agree with or embrace all our employer's policies or all the behaviors of our co-workers. We can push back when policies are in the developmental stage and tell our colleagues about our moral code, which, in a nutshell, is following the teachings of the Bible as a way to happiness and fulfillment.

We are entitled to opinions, and God may put us in specific places to make a difference at a key moment. For this reason, we must pray, stay humble, and be willing to speak up when the Spirit directs us to do so. Furthermore, when we are asked to participate in workplace activities that conflict with our faith, we can do the following:

- *Start with prayer.* Talk over the situation with God.
- *Study the Bible.* We need to make sure we understand why the activity conflicts with God's Word.
- *Consult with other Christians.* We can talk the situation over with our pastor or another mature Christian whom we respect.
- *Talk with our employer.* Depending on the situation, we may be able to ask our employer for a reasonable accommodation related to our beliefs.

There may ultimately come a day when the choice comes down to doing something that goes against our faith or quitting our job. In such situations when an employer's culture conflicts with our beliefs, God will call us to seek new employment. For example, one Capital Baptist member felt boxed into a corner when his employer required certain New Age training that encouraged occult practices. He eventually quit his job to avoid participating. Other obvious examples include if our employer asks us to do something illegal or even immoral, such as promoting products or services that prematurely end human life (which would conflict with the biblical commandment not to kill).

In such cases, after praying about the situation, checking with our pastor, and asking for a different assignment, our Holy Spirit-filled consciences may force us to transition to another job. When this occurs, we can be sure the Holy Spirit will be our guide and will work with us in the timing of such a change. Following God's will is always the right move to make.

Is Chip Technology a Precursor to the End Times?

Christian scholars have long theorized about the meaning of Revelation 13, which talks about the Mark of the Beast. With the proliferation of computers and technology, it is easy to envision scenarios in which the government or employers will one day require us to have an implanted chip or device. For the Christian, accepting a mark on our hand or forehead is untenable. We can't do it. Yet for believers, this might become the ultimate temptation in the future—especially if the chip is required to purchase key items like food and gasoline.

In the past few years, the U.S. government and many companies have adopted chip technology for identifying people, keeping track of medical records, and other purposes. Before I left the Department of Homeland Security, all employees needed to use chip technology and a reader to access their computers. One could not log onto the computer system without the chip. Likewise, entry into many Homeland Security buildings also required use of the chip. A few companies have gone even further, offering employees a chance to embed chips in their hands. While this certainly is convenient, it is an unacceptable measure for students of the Bible.

The question of exactly how the Mark of the Beast will play out is an open question. However, Christians would be well advised to avoid taking any mark, chip, or other permanent designation embedded in their hands or foreheads. It is just too close to the imagery John discusses in the following passages: "He [the beast] causes all, both small and great, rich and poor, free and slave, to receive a mark on their right hand or on their foreheads. And that no one may buy or sell except one who has the mark or the name of the beast, or the number of his name" (Revelation 13:16–17).

How to Overcome Temptations From Within

So far, we have talked about temptations of an *external* nature. But now we turn to temptations that come from our own *internal* fallen nature or fleshly desires. As a pastor, few things are as heartbreaking as when I see marriages in my congregation fail. Time and again, I hear the same story of how one partner or the other succumbed to temptation at work and entered into an adulterous affair. While there are many different pitfalls, the formation of inappropriate physical and/or emotional attachments are among the most damaging.

At work, we seek to look our best, smell our best, and act on our best behavior. Co-workers spend hours together, sometimes toiling on interesting and even exciting projects. We may accomplish great things as a team and weather difficult circumstances. Bonds are formed and friendships grow. This is normal and meets basic needs such as respect, companionship, and even nurturing. But it can also lead to dangers.

So, how can we work closely with others but avoid taking our relationships in an unhealthy area? Here find some ideas.

Bring God into the Workplace

If you regularly practice God's presence, temptation will head in the other direction. So, begin your day with prayer. You can do this silently at your workstation. Read a short devotion. Play worship music (if it is permitted). Invite God's presence into your workspace. Ask Him to take an active part in your day. Taking God to work (mentally and spiritually) is for your benefit.

Also recognize that God is with you and sees it all. He is not bound by your actions or inactions. He is everywhere. "There is no creature hidden from His sight, but all things are naked and open to the eyes of Him to whom we must give account" (Hebrews 4:13). Your spouse, parents, or pastor may not be with you at work, but God definitely sees you and your behavior. "Do you not know that your bodies are members of Christ? Shall I then take the members of Christ and make them members of a harlot? Certainly not!" (1 Corinthians 6:15). With God's help, you can walk worthy of His calling on your life.

Recognize God's Plan

God sent the gift of work for your sanctification, to support yourself, to help take care of others in your life, and to learn more about Him. "For this is the will of God, your sanctification: that you should abstain from sexual immorality; that each of you should know how to possess his own vessel in sanctification and honor" (1 Thessalonians 4:3–4). Getting waylaid in a sexual relationship at work is not only likely to mess up your career but also your spiritual life and your relationships at home. It is about not letting down those who love you the most.

"Marriage is honorable among all, and the bed undefiled; but fornicators and adulterers God will judge" (Hebrews 13:4). Beyond the earthly consequences of sexual trysts, God will eventually judge those who participate in sexual sin. You may repent and find your sin covered by the blood of Christ, but your partner in the affair may not come to that same place of repentance. As a believer in Christ, you do not want to have a part in their undoing. Even if you are single, the wages of sin are always death on some level.

Control What You Say

Affairs seldom start with a single glance. It may begin with a few innocent words that come out the wrong way. The book of Proverbs warns, "My son, pay attention to my wisdom; lend your ear to my understanding, that you may preserve discretion, and your lips may keep knowledge. For the lips of an immoral woman drip honey, and her mouth is smoother than oil" (Proverbs 5:1–3). Don't ever tell someone you are attracted to him or her, as this can be interpreted as a way of letting the person know you are available to take the relationship further.

Limit the Use of Touch

In addition to enticing words, you have to steer clear of inappropriate physical closeness and touching. If you find yourself attracted to someone at work, make sure you keep a respectful distance from him or her physically. Just standing close can be taken as a signal that more contact is desired. Generally, it is not professional to touch co-workers. There are exceptions, such as an introductory handshake or a hug if someone is leaving the company or recently lost a loved one. Otherwise, there is seldom a good reason to physically touch other employees.

Commit to Purity

Scripture encourages you to flee youthful lusts. Just as Joseph fled from Potiphar's wife, you sometimes may have to take drastic measures to avoid ruining your life. This may include transferring away from an object of desire or volunteering for a different project that leads you away from the temptation. What is your goal? What are your priorities? It goes to the heart motive. "But I say to you that whoever looks at a woman to lust for her has already committed adultery with her in his heart" (Matthew 5:28).

Not all of our temptations at work will be sexual. As many sins as plague mankind, there are that many things that can tempt us at work. We walk in freedom with God, but we don't use our freedom as an excuse for sin. Each of us must do our best to walk in a way that is honoring to our Creator. God will lead us as we let Him into our thoughts and invite Him to direct our steps.

Religious Discrimination

Religious discrimination is prohibited by Title VII of the Civil Rights Act of 1964. According to the Equal Employment Opportunity Commission (EEOC), religious discrimination is "treating a person (an applicant or employee) unfavorably because of his or her religious beliefs. The law protects not only people who belong to traditional, organized religions, such as Buddhism, Christianity, Hinduism, Islam, and Judaism, but also others who have sincerely held religious, ethical or moral beliefs. Religious discrimination can also involve treating someone differently because that person is married to (or associated with) an individual of a particular religion." [1]

As stated above, Title VII protects employees from employment discrimination based on race, color, religion, sex, national origin, or protected activity. The EEOC has responsibility for administering the Act by promulgating regulations and policy associated with related matters. As Christians, we may be tempted to look the other way if we see religious discrimination in our workplace, but we have to remember that rules opposing free religious practice could one day be used against us. For this reason, we should all visit www.eeoc.gov and review the section about religious discrimination. The EEOC website provides valuable information concerning religious freedoms and responsibility to those of other faiths.

In addition to the law itself, the EEOC compliance manual gives specific guidance to employers on balancing the needs of individuals in a diverse religious climate. Much can be learned about the dividing line between acceptable and unacceptable religious behavior in the workplace.

Such prohibited conduct includes (1) treating applicants or employees differently based on their religious beliefs or practices, (2) engaging in harassment because of religious beliefs or practices (or lack thereof), (3) denying reasonable accommodation for sincerely held religious beliefs or practices, and

(4) retaliating against employees who participate in protected religious activities.

As employees within a company or organization, we have the responsibility to treat all people equally, whether or not they adhere to our belief system. It is fine to share our religious beliefs with a colleague or co-worker, provided we respect their reaction to our overtures and stop sharing if they ask us to do so. Continuing to hound someone who rebuffs our proselytizing could be viewed as unlawful religious harassment. The golden rule that Jesus taught should reign over our conduct in this area: "Therefore, whatever you want men to do to you, do also to them, for this is the Law and the Prophets" (Matthew 7:12).

Avoid Harassment

In no situation should Christians ever harass co-workers or employees for their religious beliefs or lack thereof. We also need to be careful not to criticize or tease others in regard to their religious beliefs. Many EEOC complaints begin with one party doing what they consider harmless or gentle prodding in a sensitive area. People take their religious faith, or decision not to believe, very seriously. Lack of respect for the other person's beliefs is a sure-fire way to run afoul of our employers at some point.

However, inviting co-workers to religious events (such as a Christmas play or church festival) is generally allowed. It is considered a protected area of religious speech, to the extent the employer allows others to invite and advertise non-religious events. If a work bulletin board is used for all sorts of employee-generated information, it should be acceptable to post a flyer about a church activity as well.

Interactions with customers can get tricky. Courts have allowed employees who work with the public to use the phrase "have a blessed day" when saying goodbye. However, the circumstances depend on the type of business, customer reaction, and the role of the employee. One example posted on the EEOC website includes a couple who received a poster at church proclaiming, "Jesus Saves!" The couple's pastor urged everyone to display the posters prominently, so the husband, who worked as a security guard, displayed the poster at the reception desk in the lobby of the building. His wife, who worked in the same building—but didn't interact with customers or the public—displayed the poster in her workspace.

The EEOC suggests the company would probably be on safe ground if it required the security guard to take down his poster. His location at the busy reception desk could imply the company supported the message of the poster. However, the company would have trouble proving the wife's poster caused undue hardship. She should be allowed to leave it up, because outsiders would not see her poster, and her co-workers would likely understand this represented her own belief and not the company's position.

Generally, and according to the EEOC website, companies may display Christmas trees and wreaths around the holidays without putting up decorations to accommodate the beliefs of other religions. The EEOC's stated opinion is that Title VII does not require a company to remove such decorations or put up holiday decorations to accommodate other religions.

The guidance provided in this section comes primarily from the EEOC website. However, it is not intended as a substitute for legal advice. If you have a sensitive issue at your workplace, we urge you to seek competent legal counsel before taking action.

Summary

In this chapter, we examined twelve of the most common temptations in the modern workplace. We saw how three remedies that help us fight temptation are (1) remembering the presence of God, (2) remembering God's larger plan for our lives, and (3) remembering to rely on God's power to fight our spiritual battles. We looked at external and internal temptations.

We saw how prayer, Scripture, and wise counsel can help us understand temptations that come at us from the outside and how to address them. For those issues that run afoul of our religious discrimination rights, we saw how under the law we can request a reasonable accommodation from our employer. We also discussed how to use God's presence and plan for us to combat internal temptations. We also must limit touch and, with God's help, commit to purity.

Spotlight Feature

Heather Halverson

Heather Halverson works for a global leader in the insurance and risk management field as a business resiliency manager. In this role, she helps develop the company's disaster preparedness plans and works to activate them when trouble strikes. In 2017, this meant considerable overtime for her, as one hurricane after another devastated several different states and countries. The firm's many clients urgently needed help, even as the company's employees recovered from their own losses.

This tense situation became worse when management increased the demands on Heather and others on the response team. The team's personal styles sometimes conflicted, causing several employees to consider bailing out on the company. However, Heather decided to put her faith to work in addressing the sometimes ultra-high-pressure environment and encouraging her colleagues. "I start each day with getting myself in the right place with God," she relates. "I pray and ask Him to direct my steps. I read the Bible or a devotional book, and I commit the day to Him. Everything that happens is no surprise to God."

By trusting her Savior, Heather knows God will not give her more than she can handle. Heather tries to pass that calm assurance on to others, including those who are under fire by difficult circumstances or demanding supervisors. Whether it involves assuring co-workers that she sees their tireless efforts or telling someone she is praying for him or her, God plays a major part in helping Heather deal with supervisors and co-workers alike. "You can't control other people," she states. "The Bible tells us how to behave. Check yourself and recognize what's going on. Don't get sucked into gossip."

One time, when a manager seemed to be nitpicking everyone on staff, Heather felt the Holy Spirit cautioning her not to get involved with talking about the manager. Instead, she turned the situation over to God in prayer. "Spreading gossip doesn't make the situation better," she says. "It takes a lot of practice to hold your tongue, but sometimes silence speaks louder than words."

On another occasion, when a high-ranking company official pressed her on a small omission that she deemed inconsequential, God used it to help her grow. "I had worked thirteen hours straight," she states. "After a difficult phone call, he told me to 'get some rest.' All I could manage to verbalize was 'thanks,' in not the most loving tone, and hang up the phone." Later, Heather realized she needed to apologize even for her muted response. "God used the situation to make me stronger."

Heather appreciates her job and the company where she works. "It allows me to do so much," she says. She credits her job and her supportive husband with enabling her family to adopt two children from China and support four other children around the world through various Christian organizations. "My job allows me to tithe and give to church as well," she adds. The leave policy at her job has permitted Heather and her family to travel and support other Christian works, both as short-term missionaries and just as encouragers.

A key verse that keeps her going is Colossians 3:23–24: "And whatever you do, do it heartily, as to the LORD and not to men, knowing that from the LORD you will receive the reward of the inheritance; for you serve the LORD Christ."

Spotlight Questions

In what ways can you identify with Heather's story?
What action steps occurred to you about taking God to work as you read her story?

Study Questions

1 *Read 1 John 4:18.* When and where have you seen examples of fear in your workplace?

2 When have you seen examples of the promise found in this verse, that perfect love casts out fear? Describe a time you have seen that promise fulfilled.

3 When was a time at work that you applied the principal of using love to dispel fear?

4 *Read Matthew 6:30.* In what ways has God taken care of you at work?

5 What specific situations require the most faith at your workplace?

6 How can faith help you conquer fears that hinder your performance on the job?

7 *Read John 14:6.* How should knowing that Jesus is the Way, the Truth, and the Life impact the role of the Christian believer at work?

8 In this verse, Jesus states that "no one comes to the father except through me." What does that say about other religions?

9 How can Christians show respect for the beliefs of others without compromising their own beliefs about Jesus?

10 *Read John 15:5.* Abiding in Christ is the key to producing spiritual fruit at work. In what ways do you prepare yourself to abide in Christ at work?

11 How can abiding in Christ help you deal with temptations at work?

12 What are your biggest temptations at work?

13 *Read Psalm 121:1–2.* When do you most sense God's presence in your workplace?

14 When you lift up your eyes to heaven, how have you seen God's larger plan for you and your workplace?

15 The Bible says that God will fight your battles for you. How have you seen His power win battles at your workplace?

Prayer

Gracious LORD, please free me from fear. Instill in my heart respect for and faith in Your power, Your love, and Your gift of a sound mind in Christ. Show me Your care for me at work and throughout the hours of my life. Bring me to repentance for those things I have done wrong and teach me to be holy by walking with Your Holy Spirit. I rely on You only for my salvation, my livelihood, and my well-being. The only identity that matters is my identity in Jesus Christ. Continue to inform and guide my decision-making at work. Clothe me in humility and right understanding for those I work with each day. Fight my battles for me as I yield each situation to You. In the name of Jesus, amen.

What will you do to take God to work this week?

WHAT GOD THINKS ABOUT YOU AND YOUR WORK

In this the love of God was manifested toward us, that God has sent His only begotten Son into the world, that we might live through Him.

1 John 4:9

HAVE YOU EVER KNOWN A PERSON whose every movement and action captivated your attention? Someone whose words were the equivalent of honey dripping into your ears? Could you spend hours watching that person do the simplest task? That's how God feels about you. He proved it by sending Jesus to the cross. We are infinitely fascinating to Him—so much so that He desires to have a personal relationship with us, even though we are infinitely lesser beings.

Put on God's glasses for a moment and look into the mirror. Imagine the one who created you. He looks at you like a new father looks at his first child; like a new mother fascinated with the little hands and feet of her first baby. Picture God's loving eyes staring back at you. Like a parent watching his or her child's first steps, He sees you as He created you: beautifully conceived and perfectly formed. You are exactly as He intended—unique and created for specific missions to love and care for others.

You have assignments in God's heavenly log book. Today, He sent you to smile at the older lady waiting for the bus or to help the harried mom round up her escaped Jack Russell terrier. He meant for you to care for and love these people He put in your path. Jesus taught, "A new commandment I give to you, that you love one another; as I have loved you, that you also love one another. By this all will know that you are My disciples, if you have love for one another" (John 13:34–35). Every morning when you leave your house for work, the Father will put people in your path who need just what the "redeemed" version of you can deliver.

Perhaps nothing indicates love more than a willingness to spend time, emotions, and resources on another. The God of the universe not only had time to come in human form to our planet but also stoops down individually to woo us to Himself. He takes time to hear and accept our prayers of repentance. He listens to us each day as we pray and include Him in our daily lives. That is a mind-blowing thought! The God of the universe gives us His attention and answers our prayers with His time, emotions, and resources.

Love is the test of your faith. The apostle John wrote, "Let us love one another, for love is of God; and everyone who loves is born of God and knows God" (1 John 4:7). If you accept God as your LORD, you can model His example of walking in love. It's a lifestyle choice. That means you give your time, emotions, and resources to others—not just to your friends and family but also to total strangers who can do nothing for you.

God's love is a challenge. Can you look through the lens of love at this sin-sick world, at your troubled co-workers, or at your harsh boss? Leave on those goggles of love that you used to look at yourself in the morning. See below the surface of the amazing creatures that God has placed all around you. They are fully human and completely fallible. Realize that a perfect being fashioned them in His likeness for a redeemed purpose. With His help, you can show God's supernatural love, every day, through your actions and responses to each situation.

Once you make up your mind to live this challenging Christian lifestyle, you must focus on the "how" of showing God's love. Your test—at work and everywhere else—is to keep God's commandments. "By this we know that we love the children of God, when we love God and keep His commandments. For this is the love of God, that we keep His commandments. And His commandments are not burdensome" (1 John 5:2–3).

You will not be up to this challenge of spreading God's love if you operate only in your own strength and within your own humanity. It will take a lot of prayer and a ton of practice. The good news is that God Himself wants nothing more than to have an all-day, every day, relationship with you. Talking it over with the Almighty will bring the guidance you need to handle any situation. He will show you how to be a sower of love. "Trust in the LORD with all your heart and lean not on your own understanding; in all your ways acknowledge Him, and He shall direct your paths" (Proverbs 3:5–6). God wants to show you the right way.

Serve God Through Your Work

God is a worker, and He created us in His worker image. "In the beginning God created the heavens and the earth" (Genesis 1:1). As workers, we find a sense of satisfaction and gratification through work that only it can provide. Whether it comes from mowing the lawn, tending a garden, or negotiating a successful business deal, our human DNA is wired to glean fulfillment from work.

From the beginning, God's vision for the earth included men and women who would care for the land, the animals, and other people. "Then God said, 'Let Us make man in Our image, according to Our likeness; let them have dominion over the fish of the sea, over the birds of the air, and over the cattle, over all the earth and over every creeping thing that creeps on the earth.'" (Genesis 1:26).

Is Work the Result of the Curse For Sin?

Work is not the penalty for mankind's sin. Work pre-dates sin. God worked in creating the universe. He created Adam, and He intended for him to work as well. "Then the LORD God took the man and put him in the garden of Eden to tend and keep it" (Genesis 2:15). Adam and Eve had *jobs*. They cared for that first garden, dressed it, weeded it, and harvested its produce. God gave them this assignment before they sinned and before they incurred the penalties for sin.

However, even though work itself is not part of the curse, Scripture indicates the difficulty of life and work stems from that first sin:

> Then to Adam He said, "Because you have heeded the voice of your wife, and have eaten from the tree of which I commanded you, saying, 'You shall not eat of it': 'Cursed is the ground for your sake; in toil you shall eat of it all the days of your life. Both thorns and thistles it shall bring forth for you, and you shall eat the herb of the field. In the sweat of your face you shall eat bread till you return to the ground, for out of it you were taken; for dust you are, and to dust you shall return'" (Genesis 3:17–19).

Keeping the right perspective is essential to holding onto our joy about our work. Work is not a *curse* from God but is a *gift* from God. He cursed the ground, not the people. He made the environment of work more challenging, but He also promised to bless His people as they worked. "I know that nothing is better for them than to rejoice, and to do good in their lives, and also that every man should eat and drink and enjoy the good of all his labor—it is the gift of God" (Ecclesiastes 3:12–13).

The New Testament Model: Everybody Works

The New Testament church began with great unity. The believers realized the Kingdom of Heaven had visited them on earth. Jesus, and His way of salvation, had turned their thinking upside down—to the point they started sharing their belongings freely with each other. But as time went along, some in the early church began to take advantage of the situation. Instead of working, they went from house to house spreading gossip and stirring up strife. This happened so frequently that Paul sent an epistle urging people to work and not take advantage of others:

> For even when we were with you, we commanded you this: If anyone will not work, neither shall he eat. For we hear that there are some who walk among you in a disorderly manner, not working at all, but are busybodies. Now those who are such we command and exhort through our LORD Jesus Christ that they work in quietness and eat their own bread (2 Thessalonians 3:10–12).

Lest we think work is an old-fashioned notion whose purpose has passed us by, the Bible reminds us that work, in and of itself, remains core to God's intention for us. We don't "have to" work. We "get to" work. God made a world where each of us is intended to use our unique talents to make a contribution. Each of us has a strategic part to play in God's plan. In our youth, our purpose may have included mowing the lawn for the older folks down the block. During college, it may have been to bring light and joy into a fast-food restaurant (hopefully one that served salads). As adults, our work may bless hundreds of people or a single person struggling with a serious illness or other major challenge. Embracing God's value system means letting go of our human view of the importance of one task over another.

Meeting Needs Through Your Work

There are several reasons we work. First, we work *to meet our own needs*. Although this may seem like an elementary thought, it holds the value proposition of all work. The company or organization has something of value the worker desires, and in exchange for toil—sometimes even in great difficulty—the worker receives wages to support his or her own needs.

If you want to have shelter, good food to eat, nice clothes to wear, and transportation, you work. Even if there is no one else in your household, you owe it to yourself to work. There is often joy in work, even if that lies in fellowship with co-workers and customers. Every form of work has tasks that are less enjoyable than other tasks, but that just comes with the territory.

You may not need a lot of money to live. You may be financially set thanks to a comfortable retirement income or large inheritance. However, you still have work to do. In this latter case, your work may be of the volunteer variety or take the form of an unpaid ministry. Your retirement status may open up endless volunteer possibilities. Regardless of your age or handicap, someone out there needs something you can offer.

A second reason we work is *to meet our family's needs*. "But if anyone does not provide for his own, and especially for those of his household, he has denied the faith and is worse than an unbeliever" (1 Timothy 5:8). This verse sounds harsh, because it demands action. According to God's Word, allowing your spouse or children to go without when it is within your power to provide for them doesn't cut it. Unless we are too infirm in body or mind, we must work and take care of our own.

The third reason we work is *to meet our neighbor's needs*. At times, everyone needs a helping hand. Some people do not have family that are capable of helping them. In these instances, God may provide you with a surplus and put it on your mind to help a neighbor.

Work Facilitates Giving

As a pastor, I once spent a few months studying every passage in the Bible related to giving. As a result, I developed the following definition of obedient giving: *Obedient giving means to give at least the first ten percent or more of your total gross income to God through the local church in a cheerful manner.* You would be wise to make this a goal as you work and give. "And you shall remember the LORD your God, for it is He who gives you power to get wealth, that He may establish His covenant which He swore to your fathers, as it is this day" (Deuteronomy 8:18).

We give our offerings and pay our tithes to God. The first ten percent of our earnings always belongs to Him. The prophet Malachi illustrates this in the following passage:

> Will a man rob God? Yet you have robbed Me! But you say, "In what way have we robbed You?" In tithes and offerings. You are cursed with a curse, for you have robbed Me, even this whole nation. Bring all the tithes into the storehouse, that there may be food in My house, and try Me now in this," says the LORD of hosts, "If I will not open for you the windows of heaven and pour out for you such blessing that there will not be room enough to receive it" (Malachi 3:8–10).

God continues to show His generosity to us each day. He provides for us in hundreds of ways, not the least of which are the huge spiritual blessings He pours over us. "Blessed be the God and Father of our LORD Jesus Christ, who has blessed us with every spiritual blessing in the heavenly places in Christ" (Ephesians 1:3). In light of His generosity to us, how can we be less than extravagant with our giving?

One of the great joys of working is to be able to give. Whether it is providing for the short-term needs of a family who has suffered great loss or supporting missionary work on a distant shore, nothing connects a believer more tightly to God than giving when prompted by the Spirit. "Let him who stole steal no longer, but rather let him labor, working with his hands what is good, that he may have something to give him who has need" (Ephesians 4:28).

Secular vs. Sacred

In the modern secular world, the conventional wisdom is that enemies are to be ridiculed, defamed, and trampled underfoot. From presidential candidates to talk show hosts, bad behavior is modeled for the masses and quickly adopted as the norm. In the not-too-distant past, those who aspired to top positions in government, industry, or entertainment were expected to comport themselves with dignity and prove themselves worthy of respect. Increasingly, in recent years we've seen the opposite.

In God's view, the believer's whole life is a sacred gift. There is no secular and sacred. All ground that we walk upon is sacred because we carry with us God's Holy Spirit inside. The biggest heart for service wins the day. Our work is a reflection of the love God shows to us, and the humble among us will receive the most honor from Him. Christians who find the balance between being diligent in business and demonstrating love for others are the heroes in God's Book of Life. Those who choose to give away their possessions rate much higher in God's economy than those who die with the most toys. Speed boats and sports cars won't be of much use to us in heaven when consecrated spirits move at the speed of light to do the will of the Father.

Summary

In this chapter, we looked at God's love for us and how that empowers us to love others through our work. The purposes of work include taking care of our needs, our family's needs, and our neighbors' needs. Our salary also supports the work of our church through our tithes and offerings. For believers, every aspect of life, including our work, becomes sacred when we choose to yield to God's will.

Spotlight Feature

John McKinley

As a husband and father of five, John McKinley has worked in managerial accounting for almost thirty years, including twelve years in telecom and the rest in government. After giving into his fleshly side as a young adult, he eventually consecrated his life to Christ and found the zeal that many on-fire believers experience. His Bible became his constant companion, but in the early days of walking with the LORD, he didn't read it or study it in detail. That's when a co-worker stopped him in his tracks by asking him about the meaning of Genesis 4:9: "Then the LORD said to Cain, 'Where is Abel your brother?' He said, 'I do not know. Am I my brother's keeper?'"

From that time forward, John realized the importance of learning the Bible and being able to apply it to everyday situations. He found a Bible study near his office on Capitol Hill and soaked up the concise teachings. Over time, he went from listener to active participant and eventually to Bible teacher. John now leads a growth group at Capital Baptist Church.

Over the years, God positioned John in a work environment where he could do the most good for the Kingdom. He advanced in his career and several times changed jobs and offices within the same organization. With each transition, John kept his ears open for other believers and looked for opportunities to start a Bible study at his workplace

It hasn't always gone smoothly. In one instance, the Bible study grew organically as John and a co-worker studied Scripture over lunch. Eventually, a third man joined them, and it became a regular thing. But then management became aware of the informal meeting, and they asked the men to move their study off work property "to avoid offending anyone." This setback didn't stop the proliferation of God's Word. Through a Facebook friend, John found a way to move the Bible study down the street to a cupcake company. Sweet!

In another instance, John and a few employees started a Bible study at their government office. When they went to schedule a conference room, management approved the request to reserve it, but they told John and the others the entry must be recorded as an untitled "meeting." The rationale, again, was to avoid offending anyone.

Since that time, John has found it best to work under the radar in these situations. Although he talks freely about his faith and church activities, and though most of his co-workers know he is a Christian, he doesn't fight with management over the finer points of scheduling Bible studies. He saves his concerns for more important matters. This low-key approach makes him available should the Holy Spirit draw a co-worker in need to him.

Recently, a close colleague of John's experienced a serious health challenge, and John asked if he could pray with him. Even though the co-worker declined prayer at that moment, he told John to pray for him later and to have others do the same. John brought the man's health struggle to the attention of his small group at church. Periodically, John updated the co-worker about the prayers and well wishes of his class. Eventually, the man became receptive to one-on-one prayer. John has since seen noticeable changes in his colleague as they have talked about God, prayer, and the importance of family.

As John has spent time studying God's Word at work, at home, and at church, he has discovered that, in many respects, he really is his brother's keeper. It is a role he now gladly embraces as a follower of Jesus.

Spotlight Questions

What could you identify with in John's story?

What action steps occurred to you about taking God to work?

Study Questions

1 *Read John 13:4–5.* Who is a person in your life who has demonstrated love through his or her actions?

2 What are some of the ways God demonstrates love for you?

3 How have you demonstrated the love described in this passage through your work?

4 *Read Genesis 1:26–31 and 2:8–15.* What do these passages tell you about work?

5 How should knowing that God created work before the Fall impact your view of work and its importance in your life?

6 After the Fall, life—including work—became more difficult. What are some of the difficulties you have experienced in working?

7 *Read 2 Thessalonians 3:6–12.* Think about your first full-time job. How did it make you feel to be able to provide for your own needs?

8 If God created you in His image, and He is a worker, what does that tell you about your nature?

9 Why do you think this passage challenges Christians to take care of themselves and their families?

10 *Read Psalm 103:13 and Read Ephesians 1:3–8.* In what ways has God been generous to you?

11 Why do you suppose God commands you to be a cheerful giver?

12 This verse describes God as a compassionate father. What does this imply about your struggles at work?

13 What are some of the spiritual blessings God has given to you?

14 How should wisdom and prudence guide you at work?

Prayer

Dear heavenly Father, thank You for the love gift of Your Son, Jesus Christ. Thank You for caring about me even before I was born. Thank You for the many gifts of love demonstrated throughout my career, including Your provision for myself and my family through the salary and other benefits of working. Thank You for molding and shaping my character through the challenges of working and the occasional difficulties with other people. Continue to form me into a vessel that You can work through to accomplish Your pure and holy plans.

Thank You also for the generosity of the Holy Spirit and favor that You have bestowed on me as I study and practice the wise principles of Your Word. Thank You for Your friendship and counsel as I walk daily with You at work. Protect me and hold me close, all the more so when troubles come my way. With each success, remind me through Your Spirit to maintain an attitude of thankfulness. With each failure, call me to rest in Your wisdom, counsel, and comforting words. Show me how to take You to work each day. In the name of Jesus, amen.

What will you do to take God to work this week?

How to Succeed On the Job

FINDING A JOB
YOU CAN LOVE

*As for every man to whom God has given
riches and wealth, and given him power to
eat of it, to receive his heritage and rejoice
in his labor—this is a gift of God.*
Ecclesiastes 5:19

AFTER GRADUATING FROM OHIO STATE with a degree in journalism, I searched for job prospects near my small Ohio town and the larger cities nearby. Hundreds of resumes and inquiries into every applicable job opening resulted in frustration and no success. At one point, my father even drove me 1,000 miles to Texas to test the employment opportunities there. My disappointment grew as the weeks turned into months. I had spent years learning, and now the world seemed closed to me. Finally, at my mother's suggestion, I took a government service exam and threw my hat into the ring—or my automated application in this case—for a myriad of federal jobs.

The months passed by as I dutifully answered ad after ad and went on interviews whenever they were offered to me. The low point came when one manager said, "We really didn't expect to hire a recent college grad, but we wanted to stay in touch with the college scene. That's why we invited you for an interview." It took everything within my barely sanctified body not to jump across the desk and shake that woman silly. How could anyone have such callous disregard for someone trying to break into the job market? I wanted to shout, "People have feelings!"

I had almost forgotten about the government job test by this point, and I was holding on to only a sliver of faith. I spent hours in my room, listening to music and muttering to God. I tried not to act depressed that year when my family sat down for Thanksgiving dinner. My siblings sensed my embarrassment and tried not to discuss anything about jobs or employment. Six months had elapsed since graduation, and I was no closer to getting my first job in my field.

Nights of prayer and crying out to God seemed to lead only to more frustration. When would God hear me from heaven and open the right door? *He* surely knew where I could find a job. As I played with the turkey and dressing on the plate, my brother recounted amusing story after amusing story, and everyone else laughed heartily. Then, in an instant, my world changed.

The phone rang. I was sitting closest to the land line and jumped up to answer it. A female voice on the other end indicated she wanted to talk to me about a job interview. My scores on the government service exam had evidently qualified me as a top applicant for a job in Chicago with the Social Security Administration. The woman on the phone said she doubted I would want to come all that way at my own expense, but she wanted to offer me the opportunity. Needless to say, I immediately accepted the interview!

A week later, I grabbed a friend for moral support and headed to the Midwest's largest city. In my naivete, I got off the highway in south Chicago, near the housing projects, and made my way through a dangerous neighborhood to the downtown area known as "the loop." The man who interviewed me looked a bit nefarious, and the zip code of the building lurked at 60606, but I accepted the job as soon as he offered it. I saw it as God's provision. My first government position, a GS-5 Benefit Authorizer, paid just under $13,000 per year. I could not have cared less where it was located—whether that was in downtown Chicago or on the moon, for that matter. The job offered me a start, and I became super excited about it.

At the beginning of the new year, I began a months-long training class. The gloom that had descended on my life evaporated and everything became new. Good feelings filled the room as fifteen (mostly young) people began their new lives in the big city. Our world in the training course was a cocoon, though I didn't realize it right away. The only things expected of us were showing up on time, learning the material, and passing the weekly tests. The course called for mostly open-book quizzes and tests, so only a few people struggled with them.

After four months, a manager came to our class with big news. Trainees had been assigned to modules (work areas) within the large facility. As new benefit authorizers, we would soon begin plying our trade for real. In the mornings we would still come to class, but in the afternoon the case work would begin. At first, I couldn't have been happier. The academic setting had become tedious and being cooped up in a basement classroom with the same people had gotten old. Now a whole building of adventure awaited. Soon we would be analyzing the paper social security records of real people.

Enter other co-workers. My mentor—a tall, serious smoker—spoke in short sentences with a deep, husky voice. Management labeled him the cream of the crop in Module 7, which made me lucky to be assigned to him as my trainer. To my young adult mind, he seemed overly grim and humorless. As it turns out, he would prove to be one of my more cheerful co-workers. His mission became to teach me how to make accurate changes to social security payments using the agency's then-antiquated computer system.

In retrospect, and after enjoying a thirty-three-year government career, I have to say my colleagues at the Social Security Administration rank as some of the strangest and most dysfunctional folks I have ever encountered on my work-life journey. In those days, the powers-that-be permitted smoking in the office, and several folks took full advantage of the opportunity. Alcohol may have been a no-no, but the ladies of our module brought in their locally infamous twelve-days-of-Christmas punch and imbibed liberally for two weeks around Christmas and New Year's. I abstained, fearing I would be terminated for being under the influence at work. Gossip became a way of life for several of the other benefit authorizers, and I served as fresh meat for their stories and speculation. Overall, it fell well short of a pleasant environment for a Christian.

America's second-largest city felt chock full of characters, and several of them worked just a few feet from me. In the restroom, I met my first obsessive-compulsive employee. He would wash his face and then dry it with fifteen to twenty paper towels, one after the other. Somehow, it reminded me of a sad cartoon. I had none of the spiritual training that might have given me a chance to help him.

We worked in a building called the Great Lakes Program Service Center. My experiences there stretched my faith and taught me many lessons about depending on God at work. The experience included my first glimpse at the positive and negative behaviors of co-workers that I would continue to witness throughout my career. Several people showed genuine concern for me and tried their best to help me succeed. Others were rude, used foul language, and tried to sabotage me. Fortunately, my first boss rated as one of the best of my entire career. She looked out for me in every way imaginable. She even had the district office phone moved away from my desk, as she didn't want me to be disturbed too frequently while I learned my new job.

After only eighteen months with the Social Security Administration, I heard about a much better paying job with the Air Force. So, I bid farewell to this collection of odd co-workers and beloved former training classmates and headed off to Oklahoma for more adventures in the world of work.

What Makes People Love Their Jobs?

Most of us plod along at our jobs, either liking or disliking them, and giving little thought as to why we do or don't enjoy our work. However, by studying job satisfaction, we can gain clues about our own situation and the best path forward. The following list of why people like or love their jobs is not a comprehensive list, but it includes a synthesis of input from twenty websites:

- *Enjoying co-workers.* Liking the people we work with is an often-repeated reason for job satisfaction.

- *Ability to make a significant impact.* We all want meaningful work. Having a job where we can have a significant impact on the lives of others is a top consideration for job satisfaction.

- *Feeling valued or recognized.* We all want to feel important to the organization's success. When we do something noteworthy, it helps if the organization recognizes our performance or accomplishment.

- *Alignment between our goals and those of the company.* Over the long-term, we will be satisfied as employees if we buy into the mission of our employer. That's easier to do when our beliefs align with the goals of the company.

- *Personal development and growth.* We all want to feel we are learning something and growing as a result of our job. This could be the job itself or the willingness of an employer to fund training or additional education.

- *Being well paid.* Although this is not the primary factor in job satisfaction on most lists, compensation does matter. If the job doesn't pay enough to meet our needs and those of our families (and include benefits like health insurance), our job satisfaction will eventually wane.

- *Makes use of our skills and experience.* Few of us like to feel underemployed. Having a job that calls on us to use our abilities and experiences tends to promote satisfaction in the workplace.

- *Having a good boss.* Who we work for matters a lot in keeping us happy at work. Does our boss promote harmony in the office or keep everything in a state of uproar? Does he or she support work-life balance or demand unnecessary and uncompensated overtime to meet unrealistic deadlines based on staffing levels?

- *Enjoying working with customers.* In some jobs, our satisfaction may be driven by those who depend on the services we provide. If customers are appreciative and easy to serve, their attitudes can make the job easier and more pleasant for us.

- *Projects are interesting or exciting.* If the projects we are working on are interesting and fulfilling, we will have greater satisfaction at work. Some employees even list specific projects as the reason for their job satisfaction.

- *Time off.* Benefits may be more important to some of us than to others. If a prior job demanded us to work extra hours and penalized us from taking our earned vacation time, a new job in which we are encouraged to take our vacation time can represent a big step up in job satisfaction.

- *Opportunities for advancement.* Some of us are motivated the most by opportunities to get ahead. If advancement is our primary motivation, it will be important for us to understand the amount of change within an organization and the likelihood that promotions will come up regularly.

Signs It Is Time to Move On

One of the most challenging parts of working is deciding when it is time to change jobs. No one, other than God, cares more about your career and work life than you, and no one else knows more about you. Although almost a cliché at this point, you are the CEO of your career. If you experience long-term unhappiness at work, it is your responsibility to fix it (with God's help). The following are ten signs it may be time to prayerfully consider a job hunt.

1 You feel your potential is much greater than the demands of your job.

2 Your talents are going unused in your current role and are likely to be unused in future positions within the company or organization.

3 You sense a leading away from your current company due to their hostility toward Christians and Christianity. (Be careful, though, as God may be calling you to stay and initiate change. Every time a Christian becomes uncomfortable we should not automatically take it as a definite word from above to run away.)

4 Your employer expects you or pressures you to do things that are immoral, illegal, or unethical.

5 Your witness has been compromised due to mistakes of the past. (Sometimes a fresh start is the best way to leave behind past mistakes. God forgives you and moving on may be part of self-forgiveness.)

6 A new opportunity offers career advancement. (Remember that as a part of God's family, you are not ruled by your career. You shouldn't make life decisions exclusively to gain a little more money or more influence within your organization. You also need to consider God's will and the effects a new position will have on your family, church life, and so forth.)

7 A new opportunity offers a challenge and personal growth. (I moved from a comfortable job with Navy to the more hectic Department of Homeland Security for the challenge, adventure, and personal growth.)

8 A new opportunity offers the chance to work with outstanding people.

9 A new opportunity offers a much better quality of life for your family. (Some decisions come down to family. If two jobs are roughly equal in pay and responsibilities, a chance to cut sixty minutes from a round-trip commute may be reason enough to change jobs.)

10 A new opportunity offers ministry possibilities that are not present at your current job.

Any and all of these reasons could legitimately prompt a job change. There are many other reasons as well, such as the likelihood your current employer's business is failing, changes in leadership that have taken the business in the wrong direction, and external forces that are shrinking an entire industry.

Before accepting a new job, learn all you can about your potential future employer. Get a feel for their corporate culture and understand their expectations. Seek God and bring Him into all phases of your decision to change jobs. Pray through until you find His will regarding the job change. Ask if He has specific advice about the potential new employer or your role there.

The Holy Spirit will tip you off about potential issues and challenges ahead. This happened to me when I moved from the Navy to the Department of Homeland Security. In times of prayer, God let me know the switch to the new agency would come with some difficulties. I didn't interpret the warning as a sign not to make the change but a heads-up the new challenges would come with a price. Once the difficulties began popping up, I didn't feel ambushed. I found the rewards and impact I had at Homeland Security worth the trouble.

Look Before Leaping

When you feel God is leading you to make a job change, it is important to *look up, look back, look inward,* and *look around* before leaping into a new position.

Look Up: Ask God What He Wants You to Do

Your main focus is to follow Jesus. God knows everything about you and His intention for your life. From an early age, Jesus went about His Father's business (see Luke 2:49). You should have the same mentality. If you feel your current job does not make use of your gifts, ask God for wisdom. "If any of you lacks wisdom, let him ask of God, who gives to all liberally and without reproach, and it will be given to him" (James 1:5). God wants to give you this understanding.

Look Back: Consider What You Have Enjoyed Learning and Doing

While the past is not always a perfect predictor, it can give you clues on how to move forward. Can you remember a special assignment you particularly enjoyed that used a different skill set than your normal tasks? Do you interact with people in jobs that seem more suited to your talents and gifts? "But let each one examine his own work, and then he will have rejoicing in himself alone, and not in another" (Galatians 6:4). God is honored when you tailor your career to your unique abilities and talents.

Look Inward: Consider Who You Are

Take a *SELFIE*/self-assessment:

Spiritual Gifts: "As each one has received a gift, minister it to one another, as good stewards of the manifold grace of God" (1 Peter 4:10). What are you gifted to do? If you don't know, there are many self-assessment tools available online that can help you. Some of these tests focus on personality type, while others focus on spiritual gifts or calling. By understanding yourself better, you can find the work and career that best suits you.

Expertise: "Then the LORD spoke to Moses, saying: 'See, I have called by name Bezalel the son of Uri, the son of Hur, of the tribe of Judah. And I have filled him with the Spirit of God, in wisdom, in understanding, in knowledge, and in all manner of workmanship, to design artistic works, to work in gold, in silver, in bronze, in cutting jewels for setting, in carving wood, and to work in all manner of workmanship'" (Exodus 31:1–5). Even in biblical times, some people were more skilled than others at specific jobs. What are your particular skills? If you've learned them through your work experience, note them on your resume or work profile.

Likes and Dislikes: "Delight yourself also in the LORD, and He shall give you the desires of your heart" (Psalm 37:4). What do you love to do? God will give you latitude to find a career that interests you. Think about what you've enjoyed doing in the past as an indicator of where you might fit in well in the future.

Family: "But he who is married cares about the things of the world—how he may please his wife. There is a difference between a wife and a virgin. The unmarried woman cares about the things of the LORD, that she may be holy both in body and in spirit. But she who is married cares about the things of the world—how she may please her husband" (1 Corinthians 7:33–34). What are your family's needs? You may enjoy playing video games, but if you can't make a living at it, it may not work for your family. Perhaps you can take your passion and work in a related field, such as designing video games.

Identity: What is your personality? If you are an extreme extrovert, you will not be happy spending the day alone in your office or at your job site. Think about different aspects of your personality and how they provide clues to the right type of job for you.

Environment: "Now Abel was a keeper of sheep, but Cain was a tiller of the ground" (Genesis 4:2). What places and people fit you best? Do you like to be outdoors? If sitting behind a desk is not for you, explore careers where you can be out and about. If you like a lot of activity, you may be happier working in a hospital than a quiet retail establishment.

Look Around: Consider What Opportunities Are Available

Paul wrote to the Corinthians, "For a great and effective door has opened to me, and there are many adversaries" (1 Corinthians 16:9). Sometimes, open doors provide opportunities, but they also come with obstacles. It is important to use your network and look at the possibilities. You may hold a secret desire to be a movie star, but with no training and no contacts, landing a job would be a true miracle. For the time being, God may provide a job more in keeping with your skills and abilities. Don't abandon your dreams, but be open to taking some training, volunteering at local theaters, and getting some experience before heading off to Hollywood.

You can find a great resource for understanding yourself and selecting the right career path at www.careerdirectionline.org. Many people at Capital Baptist Church have used the Career Direct assessment to better understand themselves and find the types of jobs that suit them best.

Get Feedback From Those Who Know

A woman named Julie felt beyond frustrated. After pouring five years into her job at a well-known accounting firm and even going back to school for an MBA, she wasn't included in the latest round of promotions. As she stared at her computer screen, she considered drafting a snippy email to her boss. After all, he probably gave the promotion panel negative information that caused her to be passed over again. This has to be his fault, she thought.

When she looked at the list of people who had recently been promoted to entry-level management, none of them impressed her. Sure, Jacob had a reputation for being a tough negotiator, but he only had three years of experience—and she had five. Then there was Rene. Upper management always seemed to favor her. They had just handed her a big deal with Boeing without asking who else wanted the high-impact assignment. She got tons of visibility and even won an award from her procurement customer. Julie wondered why Rene got that opportunity while she plodded away on assignments of lesser importance.

Julie reread the promotion announcement and noticed an invitation for a feedback interview. Although she knew it would be embarrassing to hear about her shortcomings, she thought she might learn something that would help her in the future. A few days later, she requested a panel follow-up briefing and met with Mr. Vlasic, the manager who ran the interviews. In addition to his role on the panel, he supervised the largest accounting section within their 300-person division. He sat across from Julie, smiling and without the least bit of nervousness. His calm demeanor allowed her to relax as well.

"Julie," he said, "thanks so much for requesting this debriefing. I think it helps employees better understand promotion decisions, and it will help you be better qualified when future vacancies occur. Let's get down to it. I can't talk about other employees or compare your performance to anyone specifically, but I can tell you what areas the panel labeled as strengths and weaknesses for your candidacy. Is that understood?"

"Yes," Julie said. "I'm just wanting feedback to know why I didn't get selected. My performance appraisals have been excellent, and I even obtained an advanced degree."

"That's true," Mr. Vlasic replied. "Your educational background is strong, and your performance appraisals are indeed excellent. Overall, you are a credible candidate. I can see you being promoted in the near future, assuming your work remains good and the interview goes well. What's lacking on your resume is depth of experience. While you have done many routine accounting transactions, there isn't a lot of complexity in the actions you've completed. In addition to that missing item on your resume, this inexperience showed up in your answers to the mandatory questions we asked each of the candidates."

Julie scratched her head and adjusted her wire-rimmed glasses. "I understand, but my section only receives certain types of accounting work. How can I get the needed experience on more complex opportunities?"

"You are on the right track," Mr. Vlasic responded cheerfully. "You need to volunteer for one of the large projects that come up from time to time. Go see the deputy director and tell him you want to be considered for future projects that are more complex in nature. He keeps a list of people who show the extra initiative and want more challenging assignments."

The interview lasted for several more minutes, but Julie already had the answer to her question. Her current job didn't provide the depth of experience she needed. She hadn't known about the deputy director's list of people who asked for more heavy-duty experience, so the debriefing interview proved well worth her time. Also, while she would follow Mr. Vlasic's recommended advice, she would also do some job hunting with organizations that could give her the needed experience.

A Word of Hope

Remember the value of contentment in your work and be thankful for those times when your work is going well and you feel that contentment. "I know that nothing is better for them than to rejoice, and to do good in their lives, and also that every man should eat and drink and enjoy the good of all his labor—it is the gift of God" (Ecclesiastes 3:12–13).

In an annual survey conducted by The Conference Board, almost fifty percent of workers reported they were dissatisfied with their jobs.[2] They spend forty or more hours each week in a bad environment or doing tasks they find unrewarding.

While work is work and recreation is recreation, God intends your job to give you some level of gratification and a measure of fulfillment. One of the keys to that satisfaction lies in tying your efforts to a critical mission of your employer.

What do you view as an important job in the world? To those who depend on your products or services, your job may be *the* most important one to them on any given day. At the Department of Homeland Security, lives literally hung in the balance each day. The goods and services purchased helped border patrol agents detect firearms or other contraband. Transportation Security Administration officials uncovered nuclear threats and explosives in airports. And Federal Emergency Management Agency personnel located, rescued, and helped disaster victims. The importance of our mission energized most of us to complete even the most mundane tasks well. As long as you connect the tasks that comprise your job with the ultimate desired outcomes, it will be easy to stay motivated.

Keys to Find the Right Job

Let's look at several keys to finding the right job—or at least the right job for right now.

Involve God

It all begins with involving God in your job search. If you ask, you will receive. God wants to give you wisdom about your vocation. He will even let you know if your timing is right for changing jobs. But remember, He will also give you choices. He will guide you, warn you about potential traps, and may delay the timing of job changes, but He will not make the decision for you. Nothing pleases Him more than when you align your will to His principles.

At one point in my late forties, things had definitely not been going my way. I had accepted a job expecting one thing, but it turned out to be something totally opposite: different duties, a different supervisor, and different work environment. Although

I prayed for two months and sent out feelers, no other job offers (or even interviews) came my way.

When I felt that I couldn't handle any more of my current situation, I cried out to God again. He quickly arranged a short informal meeting with a powerful leader at Homeland Security. This woman went on to serve as the deputy secretary of the department and even filled in as the Secretary of Homeland Security some years later. As a result of this God-arranged meeting, my resume got on the desks of many decision-makers in the department. Before I eventually accepted a new position, I received seven offers of employment from the agency's headquarters and various sub-agencies.

Although not everyone will experience this same kind of blessing, God is well able to help you when you sincerely reach out to Him for help.

Check Your Attitude

Before you change jobs or accept a first job, begin with an attitude check. Remember that as a Christ-follower, you are called to a life of service:

> But Jesus called them to Himself and said to them, "You know that those who are considered rulers over the Gentiles lord it over them, and their great ones exercise authority over them. Yet it shall not be so among you; but whoever desires to become great among you shall be your servant. And whoever of you desires to be first shall be slave of all. For even the Son of Man did not come to be served, but to serve, and to give His life a ransom for many" (Mark 10:42–45).

This has implications for your job search. You defer to God's will. Your purpose becomes finding the position where you can serve the best, not necessarily be pampered the most. The right career move may not be the job that is the cushiest, provides the most salary, or commands the most respect. Remember that you are "His workmanship, created in Christ Jesus for good works, which God prepared beforehand" (Ephesians 2:10). Discovering your gifts and the right work for you may take a lifetime, but the journey can be ultimately rewarding as you walk each day in relationship with the Ruler of the Universe.

Evaluate Yourself

Evaluate yourself honestly and with the help of the Holy Spirit. "For I say, through the grace given unto me, to every man that is among you, not to think of himself more highly than he ought to think, but to think soberly, according as God hath dealt to every man the measure of faith" (Romans 12:3). There is nothing wrong with trying to move ahead in your profession or even changing fields entirely. But some strategies require preparation. Do you have the education, experience, abilities, temperament, and wisdom to succeed at the next level? Ask God to equip you for the opportunities that will come your way. God will lead you into the right relationships and places where you can be the most effective for His kingdom.

Realistic Job Preview

Historically, the process for hiring involves applicants providing input about their experience and education. The best-qualified applicants are then chosen to come in for one or more interviews before hiring decisions are made. Unfortunately, this process can omit a key factor in retaining new hires: the recruits need to know as much as possible about the job itself. If the would-be employee doesn't understand the day-to-day activities of the job, discrepancies can arise between expectations and the reality of working for the employer. This happened to me.

Some of these problems can be avoided if the applicant receives a realistic job preview. The employee can gather this information from personal research and by asking the right questions at the interviews. Wise employers will clearly explain expectations, the type of work that will be required, the challenges associated with the job or customers, and other demands. Getting the big picture of the job also includes understanding the positives of the work environment. Before leaping to a new job, it's important to weigh all aspects of the new position. Understand if the job change will likely fix major areas of dissatisfaction with your present position.

Confirming the Job Change and the Timing

One of the greatest difficulties in your walk of faith can be ascertaining whether it is God's timing to make major changes in your life. God knows what you need and when you need it, and your job is to trust the Spirit's gentle nudging and confirm your feelings biblically. The following are some ways that will help you do this.

Read the Bible

Every Christian should have daily alone time with the LORD. This is Christianity 101. On many occasions when I've faced big career decisions, God has confirmed the right path during these quiet times. His Word is perfect, and it contains acres of wisdom. God will lead you through the words of the Bible in miraculous ways. It is a living document. Often, His guidance will seem to jump off the pages of His written Word. "For the word of God is living and powerful, and sharper than any two-edged sword, piercing even to the division of soul and spirit, and of joints and marrow, and is a discerner of the thoughts and intents of the heart" (Hebrews 4:12).

Pray

One of the habits that separates believers from nonbelievers is prayer. We know God hears us as we talk to Him. "For the eyes of the LORD are on the righteous, and His ears are open to their prayers; but the face of the LORD is against those who do evil" (1 Peter 3:12). Don't forget to pause and listen. Prayer is a two-way street, and God wants to speak with His still, small voice.

God's character is good, and He is not going to respond to your prayer for guidance in an evil way. He will not forget you or ignore your questions. His response may not seem readily apparent at first, but you can rest in the fact that He will answer in the right time. "If you then, being evil, know how to give good gifts to your children, how much more will your Father who is in heaven give good things to those who ask Him" (Matthew 7:11). Don't lose heart if the answer takes longer than expected—but also don't be surprised if you hear back quickly.

Listen to the Holy Spirit

God is a triune being, made up of three parts: the Father, the Son, and the Holy Spirit. God places His Spirit within you to lead you on your journey and comfort you during difficult times. He guides you to the extent you learn to discern His voice and follow His leading. Take time to get to know Him, so that when you face major decisions, you can hear His input. Once you get to know Him, you will never be the same. If a job change is right, He will bring peace into the situation. If you feel a lot of anxiety, either the opportunity or the timing is probably not right.

Listen to Other Believers

While God wants a direct relationship with you, He will sometimes use your pastor, your Bible study group, or other strong Christians to help you hear His voice. "A wise man will hear and increase learning, and a man of understanding will attain wise counsel" (Proverbs 1:5). You should never be afraid to talk over a potential job change with a trusted Christian confidante, but you should also check that person's advice against what you are hearing in the Word of God and from your prayer times with Jesus.

What Are Your Circumstances Saying?

Once you've done all the above, God may use circumstances to make the right path apparent. Perhaps after a significant amount of prayer, you interview for a new job but someone else is selected. This may be God telling you the time isn't right to change jobs. Conversely, you may be offered a promotion to a much more challenging job, but at the same time your spouse is diagnosed with a serious disease that will require a lot of attention over the coming months and years. This may be a signal the time isn't right to accept the promotion. Circumstances aren't everything, but God gave you a sound mind to think these things through.

Carrying Your Cross

The tricky part of the Christian life is knowing when to hang tough in the face of adversity or bail out for something better. God certainly wants us to have joy. "Go your way, eat the fat, drink the sweet, and send portions to those for whom nothing is prepared; for this day is holy to our LORD. Do not sorrow, for the joy of the LORD is your strength" (Nehemiah 8:10).

> My brethren, count it all joy when you fall into various trials, knowing that the testing of your faith produces patience. But let patience have its perfect work, that you may be perfect and complete, lacking nothing. If any of you lacks wisdom, let him ask of God, who gives to all liberally and without reproach, and it will be given to him (James 1:2–5).

So, how do we get to the place of contentment even if things aren't going our way? Paul gives us the secret in Philippians 4:11: "Not that I speak in regard to need, for I have learned in whatever state I am, to be content." We learn to accept our present circumstances, regardless of whether they are easy or difficult, knowing that God is using our life for His purposes. In the Bible, we see that Jesus looked beyond temporary earthly happiness to the great purpose His Father had commissioned for Him to fulfill. He kept His eye on the cross and the work that His Father had laid out before Him to do.

We can do the same by examining our situations at work. Are the difficulties extreme? Are the effects damaging ourselves or our most important relationships. With prayer and Bible study, we can know if it is time to quietly carry our cross a bit further. We can know if God is freeing us to move on to greener pastures where our work life can further take off. Remember that the ministry of our work goes far beyond sharing the gospel with a co-worker. Our love for others is reflected in each customer we serve, each co-worker we encourage, and each time we care for the least of God's little ones.

To the rich young ruler whose whole life lay wrapped up in his possessions, Jesus said, "One thing you lack: Go your way, sell whatever you have and give to the poor, and you will have treasure in heaven; and come, take up the cross, and follow Me" (Mark 10:21). Likewise, we will find the most happiness when we look past the temporal to the eternal value of our work.

What Is Loving Your Job?

How much thought have you given about your "dream job" or dream life? Perhaps you tend to see possibilities in many different ideas and it is difficult to choose just one. Or perhaps you see the negative possibilities before seeing the rewards and benefits. Either way, you will do yourself a service if you stop and think in detail about what you hope to get out of your ideal job. How does it differ from the status quo?

Pray through the possibilities and talk them over with God. If you are married and your children are young, your dream job may look different than if you are single. If you like frequent travel and excitement, your dream job may include several nights per month out of town. If you like routine, your dream job may take place in the same office on the same schedule every day.

Obvious things to think about when analyzing your dream job opportunity include:

- Work duties
- Salary
- Time off
- Health and life Insurance
- Personality of your new boss
- Commute
- Work travel

Not so obvious things to think about include:
- Teammates at the new job (including volume of human contact)
- Work hours (flextime?)
- Responsibilities
- Your place in the organizational chart (will you get the support you need?)
- How much the job will enable you to give
- Who you will be able to love through your job

You should also analyze job opportunities in terms of career path. Will this new position benefit the trajectory of your career for the long term? Accepting certain jobs may look right at the moment but offer little professional growth for the future. Put another way, you have to consider whether the job—even if it is a promotion—will strengthen your resume or weaken it.

Pleasing God

An old saying goes, "If you please God, it doesn't matter who you displease. If you displease God, it doesn't matter who you please." I would add that if you follow God's plan, you will ride your share of dreams in this present lifetime. God has adventures planned for you that you can't even imagine.

Growing up, I admired comedians such as Lucille Ball, Johnny Carson, Mel Brooks, and others. What an amazing gift it is to bring laughter to others. Although I'm sure each of these funny people failed to live up to God's best in one way or another, their gift of laughter must have made God smile a lot. Do the same. Find that special thing only you can do and do it well. That's an amazing gift worth mining and searching for.

Summary

By examining the factors that cause people to love their jobs, we can reverse-engineer the process of finding a job we can love. Factors such as enjoying co-workers, making an impact, feeling valued, and having opportunities for growth may overshadow salary in importance to us. Some job changes are all about quality of life issues, such as dramatically shortening a commute or reducing the stress associated with being a supervisor.

Many factors go into finding a pleasant work life and avoiding a job we dread. Having a great boss can definitely make all the difference. We need to look carefully before leaping from one opportunity to the next. This includes taking a S E L F I E to examine our Spiritual gifts, Expertise, Likes/dislikes, Family needs, Identity, and Environment. The ten ways to know it may be time to change jobs should also be helpful. If we have a specific job in mind, we should get a realistic job preview. It all comes down to finding a place where we can love others and please God.

Spotlight Feature

Stacy Vickers

Stacy Vickers, a fifth-grade science teacher working in an afflu-
ent Washington, DC, suburb, has a job she loves. Each day
represents another opportunity for her to let God's love shine
to her students and co-workers. She doesn't just work for the
paycheck but finds her divine mission in caring for the world
by teaching science.

Growing up, Stacy recalls three science teachers who were
instrumental to her decision to pursue a career in that field.
Their encouragement and even-handed presentation of scientific
facts gave her the drive to succeed at doing the same thing. Her
love of education and passion to glorify God through teaching
keeps her motivated during the many weeks that require more
than forty hours of effort.

While Stacy doesn't necessarily agree with everything written
in current textbooks, she has never felt pressured to teach theo-
ries as facts or dissuade students from their faith. "God is very
present in school," she says. She sees evidence of His working
just about every day.

Stacy teaches her students Christian values such as caring
for each other, the importance of the family, and knowing the

limitations of scientific knowledge. Occasionally, a parent will see Stacy's faith shining through, like the mother who point-blank asked her, "Are you a Christian?" When Stacy replied that she believed in Jesus, the parent teared up and told her how much she had prayed for her child to have Christian teachers.

"Public schools need to be free of religious bias," Stacy asserts. She is actually glad that proselytizing is prohibited, because she wouldn't want a teacher of another religion trying to influence her children into a different faith. "I believe public schools are not the primary place for children to learn about God and the Bible," she says. "Parents need to be teaching their own children about God and bringing them to church." Her one piece of advice is for parents is to talk to their kids about Jesus and let them see their struggles and successes as Christians. "If you don't teach them about God," she states, "how will they know?"

Fellow believers have asked Stacy whether her Christian beliefs put her at odds with the science curriculum, but fortunately this is not the case. While there are isolated issues, most of the curriculum Stacy teaches is agnostic to religion. She is also one of several voices who provides input into setting up the science curriculum. "When students ask me what I feel about evolution or creation science," she says, "I first send them back to their parents—as the school district suggests." If the student persists in knowing Stacy's opinion, she answers the child's question within her legal right.

Scripture and prayer are Stacy's primary weapons at school. She keeps Scripture cards on her desk for a special boost and to remind her of her primary purpose. She prays often for her students and co-workers.

Stacy's story should be an encouragement to each of us to find a job we can love and do well. Nothing is a better witness than a Christian who does excellent work and treats people well while he or she is doing it. Our work is a way to praise God, if we do it with excellence.

Spotlight Questions

What could you identify with in Stacy's story?

What action steps occurred to you about taking God to work?

Study Questions

1 *Read Ecclesiastes 5:19 and Ephesians 2:10.* What aspects of your current or previous jobs have you enjoyed?

2 Do you have any unfulfilled dreams about work?

3 Paul states in Ephesians 2:10 that God created you for good works. Do you know (or at least have an inkling) of what some of those good works might be in your life?

4 *Read Matthew 7:11, Luke 2:49, and 1 Peter 4:10.* Where can you go to get wisdom concerning a possible job change?

5 In the list of ten signs you may need to prayerfully consider before seeking new employment, do any of the indicators resonate with your current situation?

6 What assurance do you have from Scripture that God is on your side in finding a job you can love?

7 *Read Philippians 4:11 and James 1:2–8.* There are at least two sides to look at related to finding the right position. One side is to look for a job that better matches your experience, knowledge, skills, abilities, and passions. The other side is to learn to love the job you already have. Which side better describes your current situation?

8 As a believer, how can you discern if current difficulties represent God's refining work on your character or are a sign that you need to leave the situation?

9 Why do you think God calls you His workmanship?

10 What hint does Paul provide in Ephesians 4:29 about how to become part of the solution at your job instead of being part of the problem?

11 *Read Ecclesiastes 3:12–13.* This passage states it is a gift from above to be able to work and enjoy the results of your

labor. In what ways have you been blessed by working and earning a living?

12   How can forgiveness play a part in learning to love the job you currently hold?

Prayer

LORD, thank You for providing employment that I can love. Whether this is the job I currently have or one I will find in the future, help me to see Your hand. Allow me to recognize the many opportunities You give me daily to love others through my work. Grant me contentment with my employment and with the compensation provided from You through my employer. Equip me with the self-discipline and mental strength to excel even in challenging times. Thank You for the opportunity to partner with You in the adventure of working around me. In the name of Jesus, amen.

What will you do to take God to work this week?

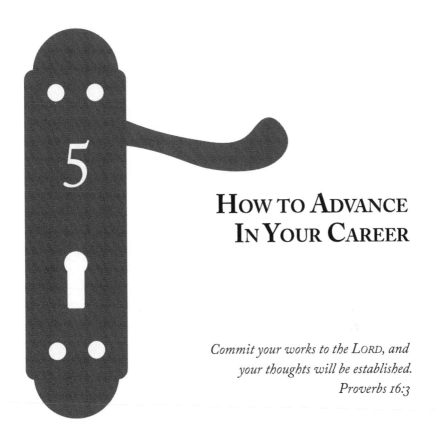

HOW TO ADVANCE
IN YOUR CAREER

Commit your works to the LORD, and
your thoughts will be established.
Proverbs 16:3

AFTER GETTING A START IN MY career by surviving eighteen months with the Social Security Administration, I continued my civilian employment with the United States Air Force as an aircraft parts buyer. For some reason, back then in 1984, the Air Force mandated that all new employees had to get a physical from their crack staff of doctors and corpsmen.

I duly reported for said physical and quickly found out a little of what I had missed by not enlisting in the military. They divided us up by sex, male and female, and herded us around like animals. The first stop was filling out a mountain of paperwork, and then we took turns getting blood drawn by a young man who didn't look older than eighteen. This young man's gifts did not include the art of phlebotomy, but he eventually found a vein. The next stop for me—along with the fifty or sixty other male cattle, still woozy from having our blood drawn by the teenager—was to receive a plastic cup and directions to a too-small-at-any-size restroom.

We were then examined by a barely-understandable doctor, who may have had a previous life behind the Iron Curtain. *All this for a higher paying job, I* thought. At the end of the exam, I was judged fit enough to sit behind a desk for eight hours a day. Whew.

After three months of training in my new field of procurement, our large class of 300 eager young professionals departed for various locations around the country. As a result of the interview phase, the Oklahoma Air Logistics Center staff wanted me more than the other available locations. When I heard the cost of living compared favorably to the planet Saturn, I eagerly headed to the oil patch for phase two of my government career.

My flexibility and willingness to move to Oklahoma transported me from an almost dead-end job in Chicago to one with more promotion potential. As I look back, I realize that God wants us to succeed in our dreams and maximize our potential, but He may require some sacrifices for us to grasp that brass ring. God plants dreams in our hearts, but He also gives us discretion about the options along the way. His success meter isn't the same as ours, but we might be surprised at how much He approves of our desires to expand our influence and opportunities. Of course, this is provided we plan to use our position to care for His world.

Six Ways to Excel in Your Career

1. Write Out Your Goals

Knowing where you are going is essential to getting there. Hope will keep you going and lead you toward your goals. It will massage your inner being after a grueling task or set of tasks. Winners write out their goals. "Then the LORD answered me and said: 'Write the vision and make it plain on tablets, that he may run who reads it'" (Habakkuk 2:2). Be specific and include measurable results. Stop at regular intervals, such as quarterly, to determine if you are on track.

While it may be possible to show up for work each day without a vision of where you are headed, it will be impossible for you to bring energy and sustained excellence without hope your life will improve. The Bible puts it this way: "Where there is no revelation, the people cast off restraint; but happy is he who keeps the law" (Proverbs 29:18). We all want to be successful at work. But how are you defining success?

Know what you value and be specific about it. You need a clear roadmap (at least for the near future), and goals can help you frame the picture of your dreams. Generalities are not motivating, so write down specific, measurable goals with deadlines to solidify their importance in your mind. By posting them where you can see them, you will give yourself hope that achieving them is possible. By revisiting and adjusting them occasionally, you will apply faith to your vision of the future. "The plans of the diligent lead surely to plenty, but those of everyone who is hasty, surely to poverty" (Proverbs 21:5). Stay diligent about reaching your goals.

2. Insist on Integrity

Dictionary.com defines integrity as "adherence to moral and ethical principles; soundness of moral character, honesty." Several of the major twelve-step programs rely on the truism that many people, even those with mental illnesses, can recover if they are able to be honest with themselves. There is a bentness to the unsanctified human character that sometimes leads people toward an easier path in life, to excuses for poor performance instead of accountability, and even to self-deception instead of honesty.

Sanctification comes by the washing of God's Word over your life. It will lead you to enduring truth—to the bedrock that can faithfully support a successful life. For this reason, you must insist on integrity from yourself and hold fast to the moral code espoused in the Bible. "He who walks with integrity walks securely, but he who perverts his ways will become known" (Proverbs 10:9). The Internet age makes these words all the more accurate.

Working in a fallen world among morally compromised people can easily lead you astray. You must remind yourself frequently that God's way is the only way. Sin leads to death, and treasure obtained inappropriately holds no lasting gain. Solomon memorialized this thought during his reign when he wrote, "Getting treasures by a lying tongue is the fleeting fantasy of those who seek death" (Proverbs 21:6). Holding fast to the integrity that comes from your heart relationship with Jesus can and will lead to completion of the Father's work in you.

3. Resist Laziness

As we mentioned in the chapter on temptations, diligence is required for success. Just about every get-rich-quick scheme implies or flatly claims its followers will soon be rich if they just do a couple of simple things. Truthfully, the only sure way to financial stability is to make smart decisions again and again.

Realize that work is good and thank God for each day you have a job. Do your work with diligence and never be lazy. The book of Proverbs puts it this way: "The soul of a lazy man desires, and has nothing; but the soul of the diligent shall be made rich" (Proverbs 13:4). God wants to increase your net worth, but it isn't the only thing on His mind. He wants to teach you His principles, and then He wants to show others around you the blessings that result when a life is surrendered to Him.

Don't get caught in the trap of being all talk and no action. Any plan is only as good as its execution. You earn by doing.

Planning is good, but a lot of hard work will also be necessary for you to be successful. Have you met people who are all talk and no action? We all have known them. This personality type existed long ago in the time of King Solomon. "In all labor there is profit, but idle chatter leads only to poverty" (Proverbs 14:23).

Lazy people come up with all kinds of excuses and often shift the blame. If you find your conditions are never right to get to work, you may be suffering from perpetual laziness. "The lazy man says, 'There is a lion in the road! A fierce lion is in the streets!' As a door turns on its hinges, so does the lazy man on his bed" (Proverbs 26:13–14).

4. Never Stop Growing

Lifelong learning is one of those buzz phrases that may or may not excite you, but the wisdom behind it is timeless. Truthfully, those of us who read God's Word knew this truism years before corporate America started talking about it. "The heart of him who has understanding seeks knowledge, but the mouth of fools feeds on foolishness" (Proverbs 15:14). Think about solutions to your company's issues, not just the problems. Potential solutions will guide you to more learning. If you are willing to find the right solution, you will be rewarded.

Perhaps you've known some older folks who seemed to go from vibrant to irrelevant. Although they had no diagnosed diminished mental capabilities, they just didn't seem to be engaged in life. If you try to talk to them about anything, they have nothing to say. If you query their opinion, they indicate they just don't know. I've left some visits with older relatives and friends feeling sad, because it was obvious they had ceased to learn or care about current events, new technologies, or new ways to help others.

Keep learning. Keep growing. Keep finding new ways to help your fellow man. "The heart of the prudent acquires knowledge, and the ear of the wise seeks knowledge" (Proverbs 18:15). Here are some ways you can continue to grow:

- *Grow through the Bible.* "He who despises the word will be destroyed, but he who fears the commandment will be rewarded" (Proverbs 13:13). The Bible contains thousands of lessons that will help you at work.

- *Grow through mentors.* "Without counsel, plans go awry, but in the multitude of counselors they are established" (Proverbs 15:22). Walking with smart people in your life will give you the benefit of their experience.

- *Grow through adversity.* "If you faint in the day of adversity, your strength is small" (Proverbs 24:10). Embrace challenges and recognize they are making you stronger.

- *Grow through critics.* "Poverty and shame will come to him who disdains correction, but he who regards a rebuke will be honored" (Proverbs 13:18). People who learn from criticism get better at their jobs.

- *Grow through mistakes.* "He who covers his sins will not prosper, but whoever confesses and forsakes them will have mercy." (Proverbs 28:13). We all fail at times. Learn the lessons from your failures and move forward.

5. Use Your Time Effectively

Although life can seem long at times, the truth is we all are a vapor and grass quickly fading. For this reason, it is important to figure out how to most effectively use your time. "So teach us to number our days, that we may gain a heart of wisdom" (Psalm 90:12). By budgeting your time, you will become intentional about how you spend it.

Winners closely manage their time. "Trust in the LORD with all your heart, and lean not on your own understanding; in all your ways acknowledge Him, and He shall direct your paths" (Proverbs 3:5–6). God will help you make decisions about your time management. It is a sin to waste your time, because to waste your time is to waste your life. "He who is slothful in his work Is a brother to him who is a great destroyer" (Proverbs 18:9).

6. Resist the Temptation to Quit

God wants you to make it to the end, and He will help you every day to do your best. He will find ways to rejuvenate you. You just have to remain open to trying new things. One of the big secrets of success is to keep trying no matter what obstacles get in your way.

Nick Foles, a perennial backup quarterback, lived out this lesson on national television when he led the Philadelphia Eagles to a win in the 2018 Super Bowl. Foles had spent his career moving from team to team, and he considered quitting several times. But by hanging in there, he put himself in a position to succeed during the 2017–2018 season.

Foles was promoted to starting quarterback when Carson Wentz suffered an injury at the end of the regular season. Foles earned a storybook ending to his year when he played well enough in the playoffs to make it to the Super Bowl and win the biggest prize in football. However, more important than his success on the field, he played a major part in the spiritual revival that swept through the Eagles' locker room. Several players accepted Christ and were baptized during the course of the season. Their witness on television and in print spoke volumes during their playoff run and eventual Super Bowl win.

Everyone falls down. Everyone makes mistakes. And most of us lose our way sometimes. "For a righteous man may fall seven times and rise again, but the wicked shall fall by calamity" (Proverbs 24:16). But the key is to never quit. With God's help, those who pay the price and keep paying it will eventually break through to a measure of success. So, when you fall down, get up and dust yourself off. Remember that others have survived what you are facing, and God can—and will—make you successful if you don't give up.

Winners are not perfect, but they are persistent. "The lazy man does not roast what he took in hunting, but diligence is man's precious possession" (Proverbs 12:27).

Long-term Success

Time and again the Bible teaches about the value of sustained effort. Your career is more like a marathon than a 100-meter dash. Get-rich-quick schemes seldom succeed, but by investing in your education, experience, and character, you increase the likelihood you will achieve your career goals. Sustained excellence won't come exclusively from your God-given gifts and experience. However, it will come as you refine those gifts and learn to bring along the Master Teacher as you practice your profession or skill.

Do the Right Thing for God

Do the right things at work because you respect God and trust His reward system. Believe it or not, others are looking to you for spiritual leadership. They stand by, hoping you are for real and your morality is based on a compass that doesn't fail. Demonstrate God's love and care in all that you do at work. People will judge your character not by the image you portray but by the actions you demonstrate.

God looks on the inside, beyond the façade, and knows your true character. He sees your thoughts and understands your motives. He told Samuel, "The LORD does not see as man sees; for man looks at the outward appearance, but the LORD looks at the heart" (1 Samuel 16:7). As you take God to work, you will conform your inward man and your outward actions to His Word as revealed in the Bible.

Invest in People

Getting to know, understand, and help other people is rarely a waste of time. Relationships lead to results. Every action you take to help someone is a deposit into your relationship bank. Someday, you may need a job recommendation, a tip on a job opening, or support for a promotion. Putting time and energy into others always pays off, even if it only helps the other person. The gold of life is knowing you've helped someone else, and it's a deposit you never need to worry about. Other investments may turn south or evaporate with inflation, but partnership with your colleagues and bosses will always be safe in the bank of goodwill.

When you look back at your career, you should have a lot of people to thank. None of us made it all on our own. Remember to practice gratitude for those who contributed to the tapestry of your career—the boss who recognized your potential, the colleague who comforted you when you made a mistake, or the customer who gave you a chance by placing a large order.

God Is Okay With Happiness

Time invested in figuring out what career or job best suits you will be time well spent. The investment will lead to your happiness, and your contentment, in turn, will lead to creativity, ambition, and commitment. If you love your job and the rewards it brings, you will be more likely to give it your all. Sometimes, Christians feel that piety requires an arms-length relationship with happiness. If you like anything too much, it must not be God's will. The opposite is actually true. Joy is invigorating and strength-producing. While the Bible espouses the benefits of delayed gratification, it also indicates tremendous blessings lie in store for those who consistently follow God's principles.

When Success Seems Slow in Coming

At times, we all feel overlooked at work. Advancement seems to come for one person or another but always seems to pass us by. Even though we are doing the right things and working as unto the LORD, the promotion goes to someone else. This is the exact hour to call out to the LORD in prayer.

Several times during my government career, I almost gave in to envying a co-worker who seemed to be finding more favor than me. Then I went into the House of the LORD, either literally (church) or figuratively (prayer). God often responded with a question, just as He does in the Bible. Here are some of the questions God asked me when I didn't get the promotion

I was hoping to get. See if any of God's simple questions to me apply to your situations relating to a co-worker moving up to a higher position.

- Did you work as hard as your co-worker?
- Would you want to deal with the manager (or customer) who came with that promotion?
- Could it be your time to be picked hasn't arrived yet?
- Is it possible that I (God) have something much better waiting for you?
- Is it okay with you that I chose to bless your co-worker with this promotion?

On the occasions I felt passed over, God brought answers to my questions. The recurring theme in all my gentle rebuffs from the LORD was that He knew what was best for me and the opportunity did not fit that description. I believe the Father shared His heart with me partly because I asked Him to do so but also because I stayed in His Word and studied the Bible. This gave Him an avenue to speak back to me.

By the end of my career, I didn't even apply for promotions until I had thoroughly prayed through about the cost of each move up and God's plan for me personally. God had taught me over the years to more accurately assess my own readiness and willingness to accept additional responsibilities. As it existed, my job by that point required me to be involved in or review the largest procurements in the Department of Homeland Security, which spent upward of six billion dollars each year. My division alone often spent more than a billion dollars a year. My jobs as division director and, eventually, chief of staff gave me plenty of challenges, chances to love people, and opportunities to be in the spotlight.

When Things Are Going Well

Life for believers should not be one big struggle. Each of us goes through periods of success where God blesses us, we get the promotion, or we receive a bonus. The bills are all paid, and we have money to spare. Things are going well at work, everyone is thriving at home, and even the family dog seems to be behaving himself. In these happy times, make sure to stay in God's Word and pray during the times of peace and quiet. Remember to be thankful for all the blessings that come your way.

Part of the road to advancement is being able to handle success. Once you get the promotion, redouble your efforts to serve and love everyone through the added responsibilities. Our freedom in Christ is an amazing gift. "For you, brethren, have been called to liberty; only do not use liberty as an opportunity for the flesh, but through love serve one another" (Galatians 5:13). Once you get ahead, don't let down your guard and get off track. Many good men and women have swelled with pride following a big promotion, and these same people have taken tremendous falls as a result.

Poise Looks Good on Everyone

Reactions to a promotion say a lot about you and your maturity level. Do it right, and even your enemies will cheer for you. Do it wrong, and even the one who promotes you will regret it. As always, a humble spirit looks good on everyone. Keep in mind that your boss promoted you because he or she deemed you able to handle additional responsibilities with poise. In biblical parlance, that means being a servant with broader responsibilities. More people to serve. More responsibilities under your ownership.

Internalize the good feelings of being the one selected. Celebrate and be thankful. But realize that while your number came up this time, next time you may be the one congratulating someone else. As you accept new responsibilities, remember that some of your co-workers may feel stuck in their careers. Your advancement may bring up certain feelings for them, such as resentment and jealousy.

Likewise, react well to your rivals and colleagues when they are promoted and when they face difficult times. "Do not rejoice when your enemy falls, and do not let your heart be glad when he stumbles" (Proverbs 24:17). When one of my co-workers faced demotion, I hurried in to offer her a job in my division. Although she chose a different opportunity, I made a friend for life. People remember how you treat them in good times, but they remember it more when they are facing tough times. Give people a soft landing place when it is their turn to fall. They just might do the same for you later.

When You Feel Stuck

From time to time, it may feel as if you are stuck at a certain level in your career. God wants to hear all of your thoughts, and it's perfectly fine to bring this concern to Him. "The wise shall inherit glory: but shame shall be the legacy of fools" (Proverbs 3:35). While it makes no sense to throw away a perfectly good job that provides for you and/or your family, it's worth taking time to examine why you feel dissatisfied. Is it repetitive tasks? Is it a lack of promotion potential in your field? Is it unpleasant aspects of your job? Beyond staying in faith that God is watching out for you, it may be helpful to look inside during those times. Here are five ways you can do this when you feel stuck in your career.

1. Determine Your Level of Interest

Determine if you are passionate about your current job, company, or work environment. Most of us find it difficult to succeed if we really don't like what we do, so ask yourself whether the daily tasks are consistent with your personality. For instance, if you hate conflict, you shouldn't be in a position where negotiating contentious issues between the union and management is a major part of your job. In addition, consider whether the mission of your company or organization is consistent with your values and interests. For example, if you don't think plastic bags are good for the environment and that is something you care about deeply, you shouldn't be working for company that makes plastic bags.

2. Get Real With Yourself

Get real with yourself about your level of knowledge, skill, and ability. Ask God to show you what you might be lacking to move ahead, and then pay attention. God will bring up situations and conversations that will help you know what areas to work on, whether it is more experience, training, education, or people skills. Research what credentials are important at the next level in your field and ask yourself if you possess that degree, certification, or experience.

3. Ask Your Boss for Feedback

Ask your boss for feedback about your performance—and don't be thin-skinned about the answers. Most organizations have a regular performance review process, so use it to your advantage. Probe deeper. Don't settle for platitudes such as, "Oh, you're doing okay." Ask what things you could do to increase your chances of being considered for a promotion. How can you improve? Are there special projects that could prepare you for promotion down the line?

4. Test the Marketplace

If you believe there is a better job out there for you, test the marketplace. Whether you find another job or not, it will give you a better understanding of the possibilities out there given your current qualifications. (Of course, if at all possible, be sure to secure the next job before quitting your current one.) As a manager, it used to drive me mildly crazy when employees had an exaggerated sense of their own salary potential. The market is seldom wrong. So, get out there and apply for other jobs if you think you are sorely underpaid. If you don't get offers, try to follow up and find out anything that is missing from your background.

5. Do Your Best Every Day

Until you get promoted or find a new job, do your best every day. Managers are not impressed by words; it's all about action. If you start consistently doing excellent work, on time and under budget, opportunities for advancement should eventually come your way.

Give Your Career to God

Previously, I mentioned that in my search for career advancement, I took a job with the Air Force in Oklahoma in 1984. Being raised in Ohio, and coming from Chicago at the time, the move to oil country came with a great deal of culture shock. While all people have things in common, the Oklahoma mindset of that day took some getting used to.

For example, pick-up trucks populated every parking lot. Not a *few* pick-up trucks, but many, many, pick-up trucks. This often led me to park in tight quarters between two behemoth vehicles. I would have to squeeze out of my compact car while trying not bump the extended-cab truck next to me for fear a gun-toting Okie might open fire before I could make it safely into the store. (I exaggerate only slightly.)

Another example of the differences was that my neighbor in the apartment building where I lived had a live wolf as a pet. Not a small, hybrid dog/wolf, but a real, big wolf with fangs and a menacing attitude. My neighbor brought it over to my apartment to show me once, complete with a heavy chain around the animal's neck. I have trouble relating to people with pets that could devour me.

Apart from the broad cultural differences, the Air Force work environment felt different than the one at the Social Security Administration. Several of the long-time Air Force employees worried that all the new trainees from our hiring class would get promoted ahead of them, even though they had more seniority. This led some of the trainers to be less than hospitable.

The biggest issue with my Oklahoma job turned out to be the work itself, as the negotiations required in the position didn't fit well with my personality. I don't like conflict. My job with the Air Force involved negotiating prices on aircraft parts. In most cases, the government did not own the rights to the drawings for these particular aircraft parts, and the defense contractors who owned the proprietary rights did not prove eager to give price breaks.

The companies, like Boeing and General Electric, knew they were the only authorized supplier and the only ones legally permitted to produce and sell the parts. This gave them the upper hand in negotiations. So, my job involved calling people who didn't want to hear from me and argue with them in an attempt to get cheaper prices.

Turning My Work Life Over to God

Finally, I came to the end of myself and cried out to the LORD. I prayed that God would take over my career and show me the right way to go. My best efforts had left me miserable, unfulfilled, and sitting in a large aircraft hangar in Oklahoma. It proved to be an emotional bottom for me. Coming to the end of myself and asking God to take over became the smartest decision I ever made. I realized that just being a Christian wasn't enough. If I didn't let God control my life, I would give up many of the benefits of my relationship with the Ruler of the Universe.

This amounted to a watershed moment. From that time on, God took over the control of my career. Within a few months, a friend told me about an opportunity in Chicago with the Navy. I didn't have to completely change fields or leave procurement, but I was able to go from difficult negotiations with large companies to administering research contracts and grants with universities. The position in Chicago had greater promotion potential than in Oklahoma, and it put me within driving distance of my parents in Ohio. This allowed me to buzz home for an occasional weekend visit, which proved increasingly precious as my dad's health deteriorated.

"Commit your works to the LORD, and your thoughts will be established" (Proverbs 16:3). I certainly found this to be true in my life. While there were still challenges and periods of difficulty, overall the intense struggles subsided when I turned my work life over to God. The last twenty-eight years of my career unfolded much easier than the first five years. All I had to do was commit the whole thing to God and let Him lead me. Try it and see if God is indeed good.

Summary

In this chapter, we examined six ways you can emulate the way God works and move ahead in your career: (1) write out your goals, (2) insist on walking in integrity, (3) never be lazy, (4) never stop growing, (5) manage your time well, and (6) resist the temptation to quit. Avoid stagnating in your career and life by continually seeking out new challenges. We also examined long-term strategies for success, such as avoiding the quest to get ahead just for appearances, investing in people, and not fearing the prospects of happiness.

When success seems slow in coming or you feel stuck, seek to understand the differences between the requirements needed for a promotion you are seeking and your education and experience. Figure out if your company or organization stirs your passion to do excellent work. Get feedback from your boss and, if necessary, prayerfully consider testing the job market to see if another employer might be willing to pay you more or offer more responsibility than your current job. Most importantly, turn your career and work life over to God. Let Him be in charge, because He loves you and wants the best for you.

Spotlight Feature

Ken Matos

Ken Matos faced a major challenge in December 2008 when his employer suddenly terminated him. Just two months before, he had left a secure job as the controller of a different company, so a pink slip was the last thing he expected. The experience jolted him and caused him to assess what had gone wrong. As he reflected, he noticed an ad for government accountants.

Several applications and several months later, Ken landed a job at the Department of Housing and Urban Development in Washington, DC. At the time he and his wife had children in school in New Jersey, so they decided he should get a studio apartment near his job and commute home for the weekends. Ken's four-day work week with ten-hour days facilitated the plan, and everything went well at first. Ken even landed a second job as a part-time accounting instructor at the University of Maryland University College. His key verse during this process became, "Trust in the LORD with all your heart, and lean not on your own understanding; in all your ways acknowledge Him, and He shall direct your paths" (Proverbs 3:5–6).

While Ken had always been open about his faith, opportunities presented themselves frequently at his new job, and he shared the gospel freely with co-workers. After a year in Washington, Ken received a promotion. Weeks turned into years, and before he knew it, he received another promotion. However, this new role required him to transfer to the Bureau of Indian Affairs in the Virginia suburbs of our nation's capital.

Although everything was progressing well with his job, the commute to New Jersey on the weekends eventually wore him down. Enter some not-so-helpful church friends, who started speaking doubts into the ear of Ken's wife. They suggested a young husband alone in another city spelled potential disaster. Ken's wife knew he was a devoted family man and committed believer, so she didn't believe the idle chatter. She knew Ken had put his faith in the LORD and would not stray. Even so, this period in their lives became a trying time for Ken as he commuted weekly almost six hours each way to be with his family.

When Ken's eldest daughter graduated from high school, he and his wife began to arrange for the rest of the family to move to Virginia during the summer of 2014. Thanks to the LORD's leading and advice from a friend at work, Ken discovered lower-priced homes in nearby West Virginia. The location was just over an hour from his job in Reston, Virginia, and he and his wife decided to build their dream house there. The family reunited after five years of long-distance marriage in a brand-new home. Ken and his family had done what they needed to do for him to support them, and he can now see God's hand leading them throughout the process.

Ken credits God for all the gifts he has received, including the promotions at work, the opportunities to live out his faith, and the preservation of his marriage. His five years in the crucible led to amazing ministry opportunities for Ken in West Virginia. He founded a dynamic men's ministry called Kingdom Men, and under his leadership, the group has grown astronomically in numbers. They are doing much today for their church and community.

Throughout Ken's trials and temptations, he held fast to Ephesians 6:13, which tells us to put on spiritual armor. Even today, he mentally puts on the whole armor of God each day and remains rooted in God's Word. This is what being a Kingdom Man is all about.

Spotlight Questions

What could you identify with in Ken's story?

What action steps occurred to you about taking God to work?

Study Questions

1   *Read Proverbs 16:3.* Have you committed your work to the LORD? If so, what are some practical ways you have yielded to His plan for your work life?

2   In what ways has God established your thoughts?

3   *Read Proverbs 29:18.* Do you have written goals related to your work? What are they?

4   In what ways have you bought into the vision or plan at your workplace?

5   How does a lack of vision feed into lawlessness at work and beyond?

6   *Read Ecclesiastes 3:12–13 and James 1:2–8.* God's Word calls it a gift from above to be able to enjoy the fruit of your labor. In what ways do you feel blessed by your work?

7   What is the relationship between contentment and overspending?

8   How are you demonstrating patience and faith when it comes to workplace issues?

9   *Read Proverbs 10:9 and 21:6.* What are some ways employees walk in integrity at work?

10   Why do some people make a habit of lying at work?

11   What are the rewards of walking in integrity versus giving into deceptive shortcuts at work?

12   *Read Proverbs 15:14, 18:15, and 24:16.* What steps have you taken to increase your knowledge of your duties or chosen field?

13   How is acquiring knowledge a sign of prudence?

14   Righteous people are known for getting up after a fall. Why do you think people of faith have more staying power?

Prayer

Dear Father, we know that You lift up leaders and take them down, in accordance with Your great plans. I ask that You make me the best Christian possible, so that I can be used for Your purposes. Grant me a right view of myself and my work. Let me not be lifted up with pride or stooped down by false humility. Show me the way of diligence, patience, and commitment related to my duties. Help me, through Your Holy Spirit, to walk in integrity, eschew evil, and embrace good. Fill me with knowledge and wisdom, so I may be prepared for advancement if that is the best course of action for myself and for Your plan. Finally, let me turn to You in times of great success and in times of failure, knowing You are my source and my protector. In the name of Jesus, amen.

What will you do to take God to work this week?

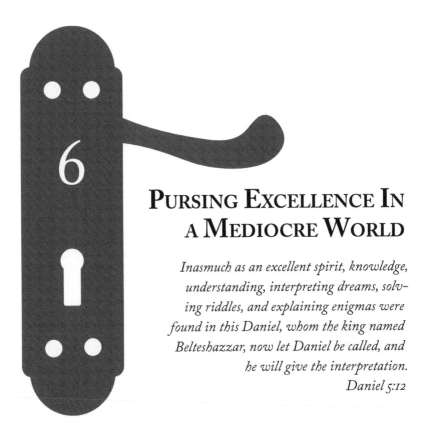

6

PURSING EXCELLENCE IN A MEDIOCRE WORLD

Inasmuch as an excellent spirit, knowledge, understanding, interpreting dreams, solving riddles, and explaining enigmas were found in this Daniel, whom the king named Belteshazzar, now let Daniel be called, and he will give the interpretation.

Daniel 5:12

DANIEL HAD EVERY RIGHT to shut down emotionally. His homeland had been conquered, and he was living in exile in a foreign capital. His life had been turned upside down, and everything about his outward circumstances had changed for the worse. If anyone could have felt entitled to phone in his performance, it was Daniel. He could have lived out his life a disgruntled prisoner, doing the minimum for his captors. Instead, he kept praying three times a day, kept believing God remained in control, and kept using his gifts to help others. Over the years in Babylon, he developed a reputation among his captors for sustained excellence.

Many of us face similar challenges and similar opportunities for disillusionment. Perhaps we spent a lot of time building a strong track record with our boss, only to see that boss accept another job at a different company. Or perhaps our years of service seemingly became meaningless when our corporation got taken over by a competitor.

Daniel made his mark as a government worker. Even though his adopted country did not honor the LORD God, Daniel still found favor. At times, his faith put him at odds with the powers that be, but that didn't change his perspective of pleasing God first. His diligence proved the saying true that "those who do an excellent job will never lack for work."

Doing the best job possible is never wasted effort. A strong reputation endures in good times and bad. Everyone wants the best performer on his or her team. A persons' reputation spreads—whether it is positive or negative—and excellent workers are always in demand. According to Dictionary.com, "excellence" means superiority or eminence. A person with excellence surpasses others in some respect or area. They do their jobs well. They find creative solutions, document thoroughly, follow up, close the loop, adhere to laws, accomplish the goal, and meet deadlines.

Temporary ups and downs happen to everyone. However, while circumstances may be out of our control, winners find a way to do excellent work even in difficult situations. Excellence has a lot to do with dogged determination and tireless attention to detail. The best employees reread emails *before* they hit send. Preeminent managers carefully gather facts *before* steering their organizations in one direction or another.

Mediocrity Is the World's Standard

Many workers do just enough to get by. If they can get away with a shoddy job and play on their computers all afternoon, they take that path. Instead of double-checking their work or improving a first draft, they pass the work product along to the next person. If no one complains, they consider it a good day.

Mediocrity includes work that is of poor quality and brings about second-rate results. We often recognize unexceptional service as we see it—such as when we order coffee but aren't offered a refill or warm up. Indifferent attitudes spell trouble in customer service jobs. How long can a business last if the employees don't care whether customers are pleased?

As Christians, we are called to a higher standard and a different way of life. Our efforts should reflect the glory of God in everything we do. There is nothing glorious about a document that has several typos or a building with crooked walls. Not everyone may be an artist, but we can all do our best at whatever job is in front of us.

Have you ever spent a day feeling underwhelmed by the undistinguished products and services you receive? Perhaps you go to a fast-food restaurant for breakfast. As you pull onto the highway, you anticipate that first intoxicating drink of diet soda, only to take a disappointing gulp. They gave you regular soda instead of diet! Although it was a minor mistake, it begins your day on the wrong note. There's no time to go back and get it fixed. Perhaps you can't drink regular soda, so you pour it out, wasting your two dollars. With nothing to drink, your breakfast gets cold as you wait to eat it until you get to the office.

After a busy morning, you decide to hike two blocks to pick up your suit from the dry cleaner. They quickly locate the clothes assigned to your ticket and charge you substantially more than you expected. When you get back to your office and hang the suit on the back of your door, you notice the stain on your suit lapel is still there. The cleaners didn't get the Grand Marnier sauce out of it, and it is unwearable. You have a meeting in fifteen minutes, and there is no time to take it back to the cleaners right then.

Finally, your work day is over, and you want to head home. However, before you retrieve your car, you have to return the suit to the dry cleaner for another try. Traffic is more snarled than usual, because the construction crew reopened a couple of freeway lanes later than they should have. It is a minor mistake, but it costs you (and thousands of other commuters) an extra twenty minutes to navigate the resulting traffic jam.

You finally arrive home and retrieve your mail from the box. You absentmindedly open the electric bill, and your eyes nearly bug out of your head when you see the monthly charge: $1,342,567.14. You know it's an error, but the prospect of the time it will take on the phone to straighten it out does not improve the trajectory of your day.

All these mistakes are small matters that reflect less than excellent performance. In some way, each foul-up represents someone's failure to take care of God's world and His creation. That's why it is important for us to always try our best and take pride in our jobs, regardless of whether the world considers them important or not. Mistakes happen, but we can reduce the number of errors by applying our best effort and pushing ourselves just a bit.

Why Should Believers Strive to Do Excellent Work?

The first reason we work as unto God is because He will be our ultimate judge. Although Jesus paid the price for our sin through His death, burial, and resurrection, the things we accomplish with our talents will be subject to God's review. He will use His own value system to test the quality of our work.

> Each one's work will become clear; for the Day will declare it, because it will be revealed by fire; and the fire will test each one's work, of what sort it is. If anyone's work which he has built on *it* endures, he will receive a reward. If anyone's work is burned, he will suffer loss; but he himself will be saved, yet so as through fire (1 Corinthians 3:13–15).

A second reason we work as unto God is because it serves as a testimony to others. We don't do good just to please God but because people need what we have to offer. Not only do they need it, but they also need to know about the God who lies behind our motivations. "Let your light so shine before men, that they may see your good works and glorify your Father in heaven" (Matthew 5:16). We need to testify by our actions and commitment to propriety.

How Do We Demonstrate Excellence?

There are many ingredients to excellence, some of which we must demonstrate as a regular part of who we are and what we hope to become.

Excellence Through Our Character

Regardless of the ethical challenges of our workplace or industry, God expects us to stand up for what is right. Just because "everyone else is doing it" doesn't mean we should also partake. "But Daniel purposed in his heart that he would not defile himself with the portion of the king's delicacies, nor with the wine which he drank; therefore, he requested of the chief of the eunuchs that he might not defile himself" (Daniel 1:8).

Excellence Through Our Skills and Wisdom

Everything we do makes an impression. We have to go beyond just being average and shoot for excellence. We have to get that extra training, take time to watch that video about how to do our job better, study up on the competition, and ensure that our skills far exceed the minimum expected proficiency.

> Then Daniel was brought in before the king. The king spoke, and said to Daniel, "Are you that Daniel who is one of the captives from Judah, whom my father the king brought from Judah? I have heard of you, that the Spirit of God is in you, and that light and understanding and excellent wisdom are found in you" (Daniel 5:13–14).

Having all the training and skills in the world won't accomplish much if you don't have wisdom. So, pray for God to develop the wisdom needed for the challenges ahead of you. He will respond. True excellence is dependent on making wise choices.

Excellence Through Our Dedication

We have to stay committed to doing our best. Others may try to bring us down, but with God's help, we can stay focused on the mission. We can prove our character by steering clear of disloyalty to our boss and our company. "Then this Daniel distinguished himself above the governors and satraps, because an excellent spirit was in him; and the king gave thought to setting him over the whole realm" (Daniel 6:3).

It's important for us to dedicate ourselves to each of the responsibilities that come our way. We can't assume that whatever effort we usually expend will be enough for the new challenge. We have to pray and dedicate ourselves to successfully accomplishing that new project. "Whatever your hand finds to do, do it with your might; for there is no work or device or knowledge or wisdom in the grave where you are going" (Ecclesiastes 9:10). Our time on earth is limited, so we have to give it our all while we can.

Excellence Through Our Enthusiasm

Staying positive shows our enthusiasm. "Not lagging in diligence, fervent in spirit, serving the Lord" (Romans 12:11). It's one thing to accept an assignment politely, but it's another to look for the good in a project and show our excitement about being involved with it.

Excellence Through Sharpening Our Skills

Over time skills can deteriorate, particularly those we don't use often, so we need to keep accepting challenges that build our skills. "If the ax is dull, and one does not sharpen the edge, then he must use more strength; but wisdom brings success" (Ecclesiastes 10:10). We shouldn't run away from *all* conflict, as healthy debate about the right approach can often strengthen the final product and those who participate in creating it. "As iron sharpens iron, so a man sharpens the countenance of his friend" (Proverbs 27:17).

Excellence Through Keeping Our Word

We need to think carefully when signing up for a deadline. Nothing will erode others' confidence in us more quickly than not living up to our word. Over time, it should become easier for us to estimate the hours needed to perform the functions of our job. Until then, we should seek help from more experienced workers so we can understand the spoken and unspoken deadlines associated with it. "Most men will proclaim each his own goodness, but who can find a faithful man?" (Proverbs 20:6). We need to strive to live up to our promises.

Excellence Through Our Positive Attitude

At work, as in other endeavors, people will more likely forgive those who keep a positive attitude. Looking on the bright side will distinguish us from many of our co-workers. The apostle Paul instructs, "Do all things without complaining and disputing, that you may become blameless and harmless, children of God without fault in the midst of a crooked and perverse generation, among whom you shine as lights in the world" (Philippians 2:14–15).

Excellence Through Doing More Than Asked

We shouldn't be disappointed when our boss expects more of us than the average worker. The best employees always receive more assignments and successfully handle them. Jesus taught, "Whoever compels you to go one mile, go with him two" (Matthew 5:41). In the Bible, we read how Rebecca went the second mile when she was asked to give a drink of water. "And she made haste and let her pitcher down from her shoulder, and said, 'Drink, and I will give your camels a drink also.' So I drank, and she gave the camels a drink also" (Genesis 24:46).

What to Expect When You Do Excellent Work

Although it doesn't make sense, human nature will cause some people to resent your efficiency, effectiveness, and effort. Even those who barely try will resent you if you finish your assignments and win the boss's praise. The same thing happened to Daniel. "Then these men said, 'We shall not find any charge against this Daniel unless we find it against him concerning the law of his God'" (Daniel 6:5).

However, while certain co-workers may not appreciate your excellence, you can rest assured God will reward you. "So this Daniel prospered in the reign of Darius and in the reign of Cyrus the Persian" (Daniel 6:28).

The best performers find the spotlight, even if they don't seek it. God has great things in store for those who use their gifts to the fullest. Just when you think no one is looking, God may focus attention clearly on you. "Do you see a man who excels in his work? He will stand before kings; he will not stand before unknown men" (Proverbs 22:29).

Ways to Stay Motivated Toward Excellence

For many people, when it comes to excellence, the issue is not availability or capability but *motivation*. At the beginning of this chapter, we learned that Daniel had a spirit of excellence within him. Each of us must likewise do what it takes to develop a spirit of excellence and learn what helps us stay motivated to always do our best. This could include prayer and even an occasional pep talk. Developing a spirit of excellence is part discipline, part psychology, and part operant conditioning. The more we shoot for the pinnacle, the closer we are likely to come. Let's take a look at some of the components of motivation.

Discipline

Everyone enjoys the accolades that come with superior performance, but not everyone has trained themselves to require excellence. Habits come from repetition. If part of your job involves paperwork, discipline may begin with a checklist. ("Excellent paperwork includes *x, y,* and *z.*") By continually using the checklist, the right answers will begin appearing on the paperwork the first time. A checklist will help you avoid mistakes of omission and commission. Also, excellence involves the habit of double- or even triple-checking your work. Don't just stare at the words but ask yourself if the information is correct. Check it with source documents and make *sure* it is correct. Use spellcheck and other tools to assist you.

Psychology

Doing excellent work requires you to know how your mind works and to use it effectively. Understand your strengths and weaknesses. If you need a co-worker to help you cover your weak spots, don't be afraid to ask him or her to lend a second set of eyes to an important project. Do the same for your co-worker. If your issues occur with people, ask a trusted teammate or your boss for strategies on how to deal effectively with that temperamental customer. Most of all, understand what motivates you. Tap into your inner motivation for excellence.

Operant Conditioning

B.F. Skinner, a famous psychologist and researcher, wrote that learning happens through a series of stimuli and rewards. Some of us believe that God, not Skinner, actually invented operant conditioning. Life tends to reward us for doing certain behaviors and punish us for doing certain others. Following God's laws will make your life better, while disobeying God's laws will lead to consequences. The same is true at work. Promotions, raises, and other rewards come to those who model excellence. Purposefully train your mind to enjoy the rewards so you will put in the hard work to achieve excellence. This trait will serve you well throughout your lifetime.

Examples of Excellence

Learning to excel in your work will require you to become a student of excellence in your field. You don't want to model your work after the unsuccessful or those who are barely getting by. Instead, choose to emulate the wildly successful. Regardless of the field, some company is known as the "best in class" at what you do. The leader in quality service or superior products is doing something right—and probably many things right.

Find out what those best practices are and learn from them. Try to implement them in your world. This doesn't mean your company or organization will necessarily go along with everything the best-in-class company does, but you should be able to use the lessons learned to improve your own performance. Instead of wasting hours watching television or playing video games, take time to study excellence within your company, your industry, and beyond.

Study successful people. Understand why they have found success. Ask God to show you things about these leaders that made them the best. Learn from their wise counsel, and don't embrace any of their bad habits. Be willing to change when you find a better way of doing things. Set aside those parts of your performance that have been less than stellar.

Uphold righteousness in your work. One important difference between the Christian and those who follow self is the believer's love of righteousness. Make sure your practices in work or business align with your Christian belief system. "The wicked man does deceptive work, but he who sows righteousness will have a sure reward" (Proverbs 11:18).

Are You Stuck in a Rut?

Perhaps you began this study feeling as if your life is just humming along on autopilot. You need your job in order to survive. Your family depends on your income. Maybe you don't see any reasonable alternatives to hanging in there, right where you are, until retirement. The purpose of this study is not to create unneeded discontent or cavalierly suggesting that you abandon your current employment. But if you feel dissatisfied, the LORD may be arranging circumstances to bring you to a higher level of effectiveness for Him and His kingdom.

Like so many parts of the Christian life, the answer begins on your knees. "But you, when you pray, go into your room, and when you have shut your door, pray to your Father who is in the secret place; and your Father who sees in secret will reward you openly" (Matthew 6:6).

Recognizing God's Excellence

God's excellence begins with generosity. Everywhere we look, it's easy to see examples of God's overflowing generosity to mankind: beauty, abundant natural resources, adventurous terrain, and endless varieties of plants and animals. God knows everything we need and even all the things we want. He won't keep any good thing from us, but He might have a different timetable for us than we expect. Trust me, His timing is much better than our own. His power to overwhelm us with His generosity far exceeds anything we might imagine.

The following story represents just one example of God's generosity in my life. When I first came to Washington, I visited Wolf Trap, America's only national park for the performing arts. This beautiful concert venue includes a large covered seating area and an even larger lawn area just behind the pavilion. Acres of beautiful Virginia countryside surround the concert venue. At that first concert, I went with friends and thoroughly enjoyed the night air and the pop music. We had little money for extravagances, so we sat on blankets in the cheaper grassy area behind the pavilion. As the concert progressed, my back started to hurt, and the general lack of comfort sitting on the hard ground started to take away from the experience. While I didn't complain, my mind drifted from enjoyment to pain.

With no understanding of how the seating worked, I prayed that someday, just once, God would allow me to get tickets near the front of the big outdoor venue. Nearly thirty years and approximately 150 shows later, I have literally sat all over that venue, including up front near the stage, many times. Although some would view my prayer as frivolous, God listened. God cared enough to hear my request and make it come true—extravagantly true. He's listening to you too. He hears your secret desires and will generously answer your prayers.

Mirroring God's Excellence

God's excellence is rooted in generosity, and ours should be rooted in the same. Although it is easier to do the minimum for our boss, our colleagues, and our customers, God challenges us to do our best. We reflect God's highest character when we give of ourselves generously to those around us and lavish care on those who depend on it. By asking for the Father's help to provide our best efforts, we open up portals of power from above. By bringing the Holy Spirit with us to work, we become partners with the Almighty to lavish love upon unwitting recipients.

Motives Matter

When we consider our future, many thoughts and ideas may come to mind. God wants us to dream—He created us to dream and imagine. In fact, sanctified imagination is one of His greatest gifts. Moving beyond a mediocre mentality requires courage and vulnerability on our part. Courage allows us to risk, while vulnerability comes from the possibility we will be misunderstood. Saying, "I want more" could be rooted in vain ambition, but if sanctified, it can be rooted in a genuine desire to accomplish more with the talents God has given us.

God is on our side. He knew us before our birth. He loves us. He didn't give us so many talents and abilities without any hope we would use them. Connecting our imagination to God's dream for our potential is the secret to our success. He made us for a purpose, and He wants us to find our place among His many creations. God desires for us to maximize the incredible potential that He placed inside us.

As you consider possible dreams to pursue, let God into your thinking process. Let the dream form. Let God wash the motives around that dream. Are you getting excited because of greed, power, or other wrong motives? Pray it through. Give God your dream and ask for His blessing. He will help you find excellence beyond your imagination.

The next question ahead becomes how much work is the right amount? In other words, how should the believer who wants a well-ordered and balanced life set boundaries to manage his or his career and everything else?

Summary

In this chapter, we looked at excellence from a biblical perspective. While there is a great deal of mediocrity in the world, God wants us to pursue excellence in everything we do. Eventually, He will judge our work. Exhibiting excellence serves as a light to others that might show them our love of God. Excellence says a lot about our character, skill, and dedication. Some ways we can show excellence include demonstrating enthusiasm, sharpening our skills on a regular basis, keeping our word, maintaining a positive attitude, and doing more than asked. If we continually pursue excellence, we can expect jealousy from our co-workers and prosperity from God. We can stay motivated for excellence by practicing discipline, understanding psychological factors (personal motivators), and using operant conditioning (rewarding ourselves for excellence). As believers, we should seek to mirror God's excellence that we find all around us.

Spotlight Feature

Susanne Harrod

Susanne Harrod pursues excellence with a government research and development contractor near Dayton, Ohio. As a security manager, her job is to create, follow, and disseminate security requirements to her company to protect the interests of the United States and further the mission that her company supports.

Susanne was raised in a small-town church. She experienced God from an early age and saw faith demonstrated regularly by her mother and father. In many ways, their lives apart from the church served as a reflection of their relationship with the LORD. Susanne's mother encouraged excellence in the chores she designated to each child. Cleaning, baking, gardening, and canning made up an integral part of Susanne's everyday life. As a teenager, her father owned an ice-cream store, where his excellence in customer service, cleanliness of the workplace, and stocking supplies became the proving ground that eventually served Susanne well in the business world.

In her career, Susanne has worked for both small and large defense contractors. Her drive for excellence has led her to receive numerous awards and accolades for her employers and herself. Like most jobs, there are certain times when life is more stressful than others. Leading up to a big inspection, she might find herself working long hours and feeling the pressure to get everything right.

Susanne's quest for excellence is a natural part of her witness. She tries to demonstrate her faith through her commitment to implement security measures the right way. She tries to shine the light of Christ wherever she works by maintaining the highest level of ethical standards and personal character. She also respectfully tells her co-workers about her faith and church activities. "I talk a lot," she says, "like all the time. Any time I see God working, I mention it to my co-workers. Sometimes my words begin with 'I am not sure you believe, but ...' and then I describe what happened. I also talk about my church and our activities in the community, such as the food pantry and clothes ministry, as well as invite co-workers to our Easter egg hunt, festivals, and breakfast with Santa." Susanne uses each opportunity to shine her light.

Over the years, her job demands have included substantial travel to other cities, particularly when she was trying to set up new facilities and install needed security protocols. This area has been a particular stretch for Susanne because of responsibilities with her son, Andrew, who has cerebral palsy. Fortunately, her husband, Jim, has been able to take up the slack and support Susanne in her career. "Without Jim, I couldn't do it," she says.

Susanne offers these words to encourage others toward excellence: "I have been blessed to work with people I love and respect. There is no doubt the world sees things as 'what can I get out of it' instead of 'what can I put into it,' but I work with highly skilled and motivated people who care about others. I have watched believers go through challenges, and I have climbed some pretty steep mountains myself, but we have a light that just cannot be put out. I have been told by others, many times, that they do not understand how I can smile through it all. We know it is because there is always a light of hope for those who believe—and for those who do not."

Susanne's hope is that others can witness the light through her and someday may want to follow Jesus for themselves.

Spotlight Questions

What could you identify with in Susanne's story?

What action steps occurred to you about taking God to work?

Study Questions

1   *Read Daniel 6:3 and 1 Corinthians 13:15.* In what ways do you strive for excellence in your job?

2   From a spiritual perspective, why should you strive for excellence in your work?

3   *Read Matthew 5:16 and 1 Thessalonians 4:9–12.* How is your testimony affected by your work ethic?

4   What did Paul write to the Thessalonians about the role of work in lacking nothing?

5   *Read Daniel 1:8 and 5:12–14.* How did Daniel's discipline bring attention to himself and God?

6   What special talents did God give Daniel to use in making a point with the king?

7   When has God used your talents or personality to help someone at work?

8   *Read Ecclesiastes 9:10, Daniel 6:3–4, and Romans 12:11.* How can the spirit of excellence lead to promotion?

9   What is the relationship between being diligent and being talented?

10 *Read Proverbs 22:29 and Daniel 6:5.* When have you experienced jealousy in the workplace? How did this impact your pursuit of excellence?

II   God's favor includes rewarding excellence in this present time. When was an instance where you or a co-worker received a special honor or award?

Prayer

*L*ORD, *bless me with a spirit of excellence so others may see my witness and turn to You. Show me how to do my daily tasks with excellence and humility. Teach me to demonstrate a strong work ethic, staying with tasks until they are completed. Help me to develop self-discipline so I will not be found wanting by You. On those occasions when I am noticed or rewarded for excellent work, remind me of the constant help from Your Holy Spirit and His role in my successes. Steel my spirit against any jealousy that may arise among my peers. Help me to show graciousness, whether it is my turn for recognition or my turn to congratulate a colleague or rival. Finally, show me Your excellence all around me, and let it inspire me to do excellent work in response. In the name of Jesus, amen.*

What will you do to take God to work this week?

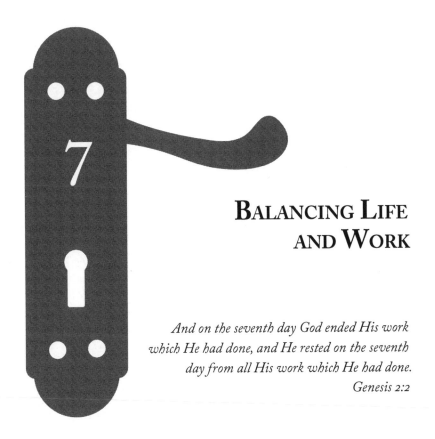

Balancing Life and Work

And on the seventh day God ended His work
which He had done, and He rested on the seventh
day from all His work which He had done.
Genesis 2:2

Thousands of years before the first business consultant uttered the term, "work-life balance," God provided the blueprint for such a life. God didn't get tired after creating the universe. The Creator of everything worked, then rested. He didn't need a break. He rested on the seventh day so we would understand how He intended our world to work. He rested to show us how to live our lives.

It all starts with placing Jesus at the center of our being. After all, He is the embodiment of the law and the prophets. Having respect for God and His laws puts us on a track for fulfillment. On our own, we can't keep the letter (or even the spirit) of these rules. However, with Jesus as our guide, we find doing the right thing comes more naturally. He gives us the love and joy we need to be new creatures at work and at home. His Holy Spirit indwells us with wisdom to know when we should crash on a key project at work or leave early for our son's soccer game. "If you then, being evil, know how to give good gifts to your children, how much more will your heavenly Father give the Holy Spirit to those who ask Him" (Luke 11:13).

Some of us know we've been on the wrong track with work. Perhaps we've overemphasized our jobs to the exclusion of spending time with loved ones or taking care of our own health. It may be time to admit our mistakes and embrace the One who has the power to forgive us and make things right. "Repent therefore and be converted, that your sins may be blotted out, so that times of refreshing may come from the presence of the LORD" (Acts 3:19).

Costs of Working Too Much

One of the more profound challenges in life is understanding the paradox of work and rest. Laziness may lead to destruction but overdoing it at work can lead to the same place. There is a point where more work only leads to frustration. Tiredness gnaws at the mind and erodes productivity. Many well-intentioned souls have put too much of their life's blood into their career or business. Instead of reaping great rewards, the harvest included failed marriages, wayward children, and poor physical health. Riches come and go, but our family should remain. They should be the ones who support us when everyone else forgets our name.

God instructed us to rest one day each week. From the beginning, His plan included rest. Every week, we need down time from work to worship the LORD, focus on our loved ones, and recharge our batteries. Getting enough rest isn't about rigidly following rules one day of the week or another. It's about balancing work and maximizing activities we find restful. If our jobs have busy times, we may need more than just a day to recover from the busiest seasons.

As a former government contracts manager, the end of the fiscal year usually came with an aircraft carrier's worth of stress. Most government appropriations expire at the end of the fiscal year, which is September 30. Depending on the dollar value and other factors, a lot of time and effort went into soliciting requirements, evaluating bids, negotiating prices, and preparing paperwork associated with contracts. Some parts of the process were out of the control of the contracting officer, such as the technical evaluation of proposals and the contractor's own review processes. When the clock struck midnight on September 30, many funding streams evaporated, and the funds couldn't be spent after that time.

Momentum built for months as everyone worked anxiously toward the award of each contract and brought in the required pieces before the money expired. By midnight on September 30, most contracting employees (both on the government side and the contractor side) were exhausted from the long hours and negotiations. That last week of September was commonly referred to as the "thirteenth month," because we felt as though we had squeezed a month's worth of work into those seven to ten days. Most contracting people took at least a week off after the end of the fiscal year. That time of rest helped buyers and contracting officers regain their equilibrium and erase some of the built-up tiredness from the months of extra hours and stress.

Ten Values That Help Build a Balanced Life

The Ten Commandments, as provided in Exodus 20, clearly explain principles that, if we follow wholeheartedly, will lead us in the direction of peace with God and our fellow man. By finding this balance, prioritizing work and home will become much easier for us.

REVERENCE FOR GOD

As we remember the transcendence of God and revere Him as our Creator, we find that life's ups and downs become more manageable. The knowledge of God is a blessing in everything we do. Thus, the first step in finding a balanced life is to acknowledge God and the value of His advice. Commandments 1 to 4 deal with this relationship we have with God:

• *Commandment 1: "You shall have no other gods before Me" (verse 3).*

• *Commandment 2: "You shall not make for yourself a carved image—any likeness of anything" (verse 4).*

• *Commandment 3: "You shall not take the name of the LORD your God in vain, for the LORD will not hold him guiltless who takes His name in vain" (verse 7).*

• *Commandment 4: "Remember the Sabbath day, to keep it holy. Six days you shall labor and do all your work, but the seventh day is the Sabbath of the LORD your God" (verses 8–9).*

RESPECT FOR OUR FELLOW MAN

The second step to living a balanced life is learning to respect others or making a conscious decision to do so. Beginning with our relationship with our parents, a fruitful life flows from respecting others. Disrespect leads to all kinds of trouble. When people feel disrespected by our words or our actions, they will respond negatively to us. Given the proper respect, even our most ardent detractors will see a difference in us that is worth emulating.

So, how do we respect others? We do so by showing them honor where it is due and respecting their lives, their loved ones, their possessions, their reputations, and their work. Commandments 5 to 10 deal with our relationships with our fellow man:

• *Commandment 5: "Honor your father and your mother, that your days may be long upon the land which the LORD your God is giving you" (verse 12).*

- *Commandment 6: "You shall not murder" (verse 13).*
- *Commandment 7: "You shall not commit adultery" (verse 14).*
- *Commandment 8: "You shall not steal" (verse 15).*
- *Commandment 9: "You shall not bear false witness against your neighbor" (verse 16).*
- *Commandment 10: "You shall not covet your neighbor's house; you shall not covet your neighbor's wife, nor his male servant, nor his female servant, nor his ox, nor his donkey, nor anything that is your neighbor's" (verse 17).*

How to Find Balance in Your Life

Determine Your Purpose

"Therefore do not be unwise, but understand what the will of the LORD is" (Ephesians 5:17). Your unique purpose in life is to discover your God-given talents and use them. Without purpose in life, you will flail along and live without direction. However, once you know your purpose, it will become easier for you to discern God's will.

God formed each of us in our mother's womb with specific purposes in mind. His plans transcend our mistakes, problems, and delays. In fact, He uses our wandering to our eventual good, if we let Him. Searching and finding your gifts will allow you to apply them to take care of God's world. Your love for others, and their responses to you, will fill up your life. God's immense intellect knows the traps into which you are most likely to fall. He not only knows how to free you but also how to keep you out of trouble in the first place.

If you consult God before making decisions, He will lead you down fruitful paths. Every person receives the breath of life from God, and He is eager to see you succeed at the things that really matter. Earthly fame or popularity is not His primary desire for you—and it shouldn't be yours, either. His mission is so much greater. If you fulfill your appointed mission to bring His kingdom to life for others, your life will blossom like a garden.

It will be difficult for you to feel you are leading a balanced life if you are also feeling you've missed your calling. If you're stuck in the wrong job or the wrong town or the wrong country, you will constantly feel as if you are missing out. Sometimes, God will let your dreams build inside you before He provides the outlet. Active waiting is the way to bridge your present life to your future dreams.

For instance, if you long to be a writer, take a writing course at the local college while you stick with the job that is paying the bills. If you eventually want to go on mission trips in another country, start learning the language from an app on your phone. If your dream is to help inner city children, volunteer to be a tutor for a few hours a week. These bridge activities will serve as outlets for your gifts. They can bring you from dissatisfaction to fulfillment, because they will prove your commitment to get where you are supposed to be going.

Get Control of Your Time

It's hard to know if your life is out of balance without under-standing how you spend your time. If you don't already do so, spend one month tracking your work and non-work time on a calendar. You may be surprised at how much time you spend commuting, shopping, eating, and the like. Once you know how you're spending your time, make subtle adjustments so that your schedule looks more like your ideal. Make changes first to those items that are most important to you. Cut your commute time. Increase time with your family. Allocate a few hours per week to a volunteer project. Get intentional about how you use your time.

Foil Time Thieves

Set up boundaries against activities that steal your time without yielding results. Leisure activities are fine and needed stress-re-lievers but consider whether you are overdoing it with the time you spend watching television, enjoying social media, looking through internet sites, or constantly checking email. Here it's all about priorities. Decompressing is good, but mindlessly wasting hours every day may be sabotaging your best life.

Do Self-Care and Family-Care

A balanced life includes the health and well-being of yourself and your family. If you are overly busy, it may require extra planning to exercise, eat right, and even get enough sleep. Organize family activities that include movement, even if it's just a bike ride around the neighborhood. Make preparing meals for the week a family togetherness time by buying a bunch of disposable containers and putting together healthy lunches.

Widen Your Circle

Whether you are single or living in a family, balance your life by adding to your social contacts. Adopt people from church or other areas of your life and invite them occasionally to join your family meals, participate in a family game night, or attend a concert or movie. Sometimes, your world may tend to fold in on itself because you lack outside contact. Just getting to know that new couple at church can be a big help to them and to you.

Whom Do We Serve?

Ultimately, we serve God. But on a daily basis, we accomplish this by serving the people in our lives. This should be the crux of our purpose for each day. Tomorrow, it may be a different set of people. Next year, our job or our family might take us to another part of the world. But our purpose will remain the same: to serve those around us with the talents and gifts God has placed within us.

For example, God may have given you the gift of hospitality. You may have a welcoming personality that is endlessly fascinated with other people, which makes it easy for you to go to great lengths to make others feel at home. You can fully operate in your gift by asking a new family at church to come to your house for dinner. It seems simple, but that hospitality could be the door that unlocks church fellowship to these new friends. If hospitality is your gift, your service in making a meal, serving it, and cleaning up afterward may be the best thing you could possibly do for God this week.

King David blessed those who knew him and those who lived in his day. "For David, after he had served his own generation by the will of God, fell asleep" (Acts 13:36). Your calling has great potential to serve your generation as well. Jesus lived this life of a servant. He knew His purpose for living and focused on fulfilling that purpose each day. "For the Son of Man has come to seek and to save that which is lost" (Luke 19:10). I doubt He found service boring. It probably energized Him most days, though the circumstances often proved difficult.

Although Jesus didn't enter formal ministry until He was thirty years old, He spent time doing the Father's will. Just as God had His Son work at a secular job in preparation for ministry, He may have a similar plan for you. Jesus also realized the lateness of the hour. "I must work the works of Him who sent Me while it is day; the night is coming when no one can work" (John 9:4). Likewise, we need to understand the finite span of our service. At some point in the not-too-distant future, each of us will be called home to spend eternity in the presence of God. This should add new excitement to our walk with the LORD.

Having Enough Time

The first words of Jesus recorded in the Bible are, "Why did you seek Me? Did you not know that I must be about My Father's business?" (Luke 2:49). Jesus' last words on the cross were, "It is finished!" (John 19:30). These statements indicate the way Jesus operated while on earth. He remained diligent and cognizant that the clock was running, but He also realized that God directed His path each day.

Remember, there is always enough time to do God's will. If you "can't get it all done," it either means you are doing things

God never intended you to do, or you are doing the right things in the wrong ways (in your own strength). Both of these deserve consideration.

You needn't be weighed down with stress or worry. If you know there is no way to do everything on your calendar, maybe God didn't *intend* for you to do some of the things on the list. Perhaps you need to ask for help. Perhaps part of the to-do list can wait until tomorrow. The other possibility is that God wants to lead you in more efficient ways to accomplish some of your tasks. He may want you to learn new ways to work.

A Balanced Life Includes Certain Disciplines

To be an effective follower of Christ, you have to install certain disciplines. Set aside time for things that matter. Schedule time to pray, read God's Word, exercise, rest, prepare healthy food, and fellowship regularly with other believers. These things will energize you to be more effective for God.

Beginning each day with a time of prayer will allow God to organize your efforts and bring into focus those activities that will make you most effective and productive. Martin Luther put it this way: "I have so much to do that I shall spend the first three hours in prayer." Reading the Bible allows God to speak into your life and will help you focus on what's most important. Taking care of your body is essential to performing your mission for God. While He may not call you to run a marathon, He can't call you to do anything if you are stuck in bed with the myriad of maladies that come from lack of mobility and excessive weight gain.

Discern Your Priorities

You cannot allow the urgent things of life to crowd out the most important priorities. "Let all things be done decently and in order" (1 Corinthians 14:40).

Imagine there is a healthy-sized fishbowl in front of you that can hold forty gallons of water. Also imagine two large bags in front of you. One contains sand and the other rocks. Finally, picture a timer and a lengthy instruction book. A loud horn sounds, and the timer begins counting down a relatively short time, say five minutes. A voice shouts, "Fill up the fishbowl!"

The sand is easier to manage, so you pour all of it into your fishbowl, filling it up to the top. You level it off, being careful not to spill any. The time expires, and another loud horn marks the end of the challenge. As you are waiting for someone to come and judge your success, you read the instruction book. Now you find out that the rocks in the bag are actually unprocessed diamonds. If you had filled the tank with rocks, you would have been rich. But now, your fishbowl is so full of sand it doesn't matter. There is no room for the diamonds.

In life, thank goodness, you still have time to read the instruction manual, the Bible. It is not too late to figure out what activities are diamonds and which ones are sand. Think about what is important in terms of the "big rocks" in your life.

BIG ROCK 1: GOD

Schedule time for private worship. "And Jesus answered and said to her, 'Martha, Martha, you are worried and troubled about many things. But one thing is needed, and Mary has chosen that good part, which will not be taken away from her'" (Luke 10:41–42). The story of Martha and Mary reminds us there is a time for everything. Sometimes, the most productive thing you can do is to stop and get alone with God. This will free your mind of stress and distractions. You may get answers to your problems during such private times of worship, or you may be more productive once you've cleared your mind of the things that are hindering you.

Schedule time for public worship. "Not forsaking the assembling of ourselves together, as is the manner of some, but exhorting one another, and so much the more as you see the Day approaching" (Hebrews 10:25). Although private worship is important, each of us needs fellowship with other believers. By coming together to worship, you will learn new ways to praise God, new songs to keep your experience fresh, and new reasons to glorify God.

Big Rock 2: Family

Schedule time for your spouse. "Live joyfully with the wife whom you love" (Ecclesiastes 9:9). Bringing joy to any relationship involves going beyond the drudgery of life's chores. Take time to delight your spouse regularly. Devise ways to make him or her happy.

Schedule time for your children. "You shall love the LORD your God with all your heart, with all your soul, and with all your strength. And these words which I command you today shall be in your heart. You shall teach them diligently to your children, and shall talk of them when you sit in your house, when you walk by the way, when you lie down, and when you rise up" (Deuteronomy 6:5–7). Most lessons will be *caught* rather than *taught* by our children. Being around you will allow them to internalize your values, your beliefs, and your love for them. Working to build an empire for your children won't matter much if they despise you while you're away making your second million dollars.

Schedule time for your parents. "Honor your father and your mother, that your days may be long upon the land which the LORD your God is giving you" (Exodus 20:12). Parents sacrifice so much for their children. Once out of the house, children need to plan time with them. It says, "I care about you for more than just what you can provide."

Big Rock 3: Job/School

"For even when we were with you, we commanded you this: If anyone will not work, neither shall he eat" (2 Thessalonians 3:10). Some people treat their jobs as if it is a big interference with their personal lives. Your work is important. People depend on you to complete tasks, take care of customers, and maintain a diligent attitude. God uses your work to look after His world.

Big Rock 4: Ministry

"As each one has received a gift, minister it to one another, as good stewards of the manifold grace of God" (1 Peter 4:10). Every believer should have one or more ways to minister to others. Your spiritual and practical gifts are an outgrowth of your faith. You show others you love God by lavishing your gifts on them—whether that is through preaching, teaching, picking up trash around the building, or whatever else. All of us have something we can do to help the body of Christ.

Big Rock 5: Self Care

"And He said to them, 'Come aside by yourselves to a deserted place and rest a while.' For there were many coming and going, and they did not even have time to eat" (Mark 6:31). If you do all the other big rocks but forget to take care of your health, your effectiveness will wane too soon. Be a good steward of yourself by taking walks, buying and preparing healthy food, and getting regular medical check-ups.

Develop Your Plan For Balanced Life

The first step in creating a balanced life is to recognize that you need a plan. A balanced life doesn't just happen; it takes thought, prayer, and planning. From time to time, it may require reallocating time to one activity or another. "And Jesus increased in wisdom and stature, and in favor with God and men" (Luke 2:52).

Next, establish your goals. Setting goals is important if you want to be successful. Even with time, you need a plan to know if you are hitting the mark. "Therefore I run thus: not with uncertainty. Thus I fight: not as one who beats the air" (1 Corinthians 9:26).

Finally, harmonize your calendar. Often, it is easy to understand what your priorities are by looking at how you spend your most precious resource. Take control and be more disciplined. Plan your time by integrating time for work, family, self-care, ministry, and rest. By careful planning, the quality of family activities can also improve. "So teach us to number our days, that we may gain a heart of wisdom" (Psalm 90:12).

Remember the Most Important Thing

Although success in business can do many positive things for yourself and your family, it is vitally important for you to keep your most important priority in focus. Honoring God and getting your family to heaven trumps all other priorities. "For what profit is it to a man if he gains the whole world, and loses his own soul? Or what will a man give in exchange for his soul?" (Matthew 16:26).

If you've been reading this book but have never made Jesus Christ the Lord of your life, don't wait another minute. Just accept His free gift of salvation. Realize that He died on the cross for your sins, was buried, and rose again on the third day. He conquered death to save you from an eternity separated from God. Invite Him into your life, and He will surely come in. Put Him in charge of every aspect of your life, including your work. You will never regret it.

Summary

A balanced life includes many rewards, just as an unbalanced one is fraught with pitfalls. The Ten Commandments provide a framework for understanding how to maintain a proper relationship with God and with others. Specific behaviors that will help us lead a balanced life include determining our purpose, getting control of our time, outsmarting time thieves, caring for ourselves and our families, and widening our circle to include others. As Christians, our lives are meant to revolve around God and our service to other people, but we shouldn't feel rushed or hurried beyond measure.

If we are getting stressed out, chances are we are doing things God didn't intend for us to do or we are doing the right things in our own strength. Living a balanced life requires embracing certain disciplines, one of which is defining priorities. We can think of these like big rocks and little rocks. If we fill up on little rocks, we may occupy all our time with less important things and not be able to accommodate the most important issues of life. The big rocks, in order, are God, family, job/school, others, and self-care. Finally, we need to commit to prayer and planning to find balance. By setting goals for each big rock, we can harmonize our calendars and allocate the right amount of time for everything, including rest.

Spotlight Feature

Sarah Reynolds Oji

The terms "Christian" and "real estate agent/team leader" used together may sound to some like an oxymoron. Sarah Oji Reynolds is both. For those who have bought and sold multiple properties, they count themselves blessed if they never run into an unscrupulous seller, buyer, or agent. In an industry where large amounts of money are exchanged, it can prove too much temptation for some who lack a steady moral compass.

At Keller Williams Realty, Sarah and her mother, Debbie Reynolds, take their ethical responsibilities seriously because of their relationship with Christ and their witness to customers, industry colleagues, and staff. Long ago, the Reynolds team made the decision to do things the right way. Sarah, the daughter of a Baptist pastor (book co-author Steve Reynolds), and her mom like to say they focus on earthly real estate while her dad handles the heavenly real estate.

As the primary day-to-day manager of one of the largest and most successful real estate teams in Virginia, Sarah supervises many eager real estate agents from all kinds of backgrounds. Many do not profess to be Christians, either coming from another religious background or none at all. From time to time,

Sarah's employees recommend paths of action that are inconsistent with the company's values. At such times, Sarah reins them in and tells them in no uncertain terms, "That's not how we do business." She knows that treating everyone right is the key to repeat business and to maintaining a solid reputation in the community.

In addition to running one of the largest real estate teams in her company, Sarah excels at being a wife and mother. Family times are important to Sarah, and she ensures there are plenty of them. By maintaining boundaries and sharing leadership responsibilities with her mother, Sarah makes her husband and her children her top priority. Time management and careful scheduling help her avoid most conflicts.

Faith and pedigree aside, Sarah admits she has made some mistakes over the years. At one point, she caught herself speaking less than favorably about someone to her team. The LORD convicted her of her actions, and she publicly apologized and asked for the forgiveness of her employees. It became a teaching moment—and a humbling one.

To keep her team on the right track, Sarah and her mother employ a lot of prayer and Christian music, which plays in the background at their office. "I try my best to be an example to them," Sarah says. Treating others the way she would want to be treated is the key to her Christian business principles.

From time to time, doors open for Sarah and her Christian staff members to share Christ. Her grandfather proved to be one of her best on-the-job evangelists. "My grandpa was a Christian who effectively took his faith to work," she says. "He shared the gospel to *everyone* he ran into, and every day he would talk about Jesus coming back. He worked assisting a realtor in my office, and it opened up the door for me to share the gospel because of the example he set. He was extremely open about his faith and wanted to make sure anyone whom God put in his path would hear the gospel."

The *Taking God to Work* message is a generational blessing for Sarah; one that she hopes to pass along to her own children someday.

Spotlight Questions

What can you identify with in Sarah's story?
What action steps occurred to you about taking God to work?

Study Questions

1 *Read Genesis 2:2.* What is your favorite leisure time activity?

2 Time is your most valuable resource. In what ways do you attempt to be a good steward of your time?

3 *Read Acts 13:36 and Ephesians 5:17.* Balancing requires scheduling time for important things. What are some important things that should be on your schedule?

4 What is an example of how you try to keep your priorities in order between work and the rest of your life?

5 Families need more than just leisure time together. What are some service activities that have brought your family closer together?

6 *Read Luke 19:10 and John 9:4.* What part does determining your purpose play in balancing your life?

7 How do you keep the focus on what's really important when so many things jockey for your time?

8 *Read Luke 10:41–42 and Hebrews 10:25.* In what way did Mary discern the moment with Jesus better than Martha?

9 Why is private worship time important as a balance to work time?

10 *Read Deuteronomy 6:5–7 and Ecclesiastes 9:9.* What times do you schedule to do special activities with your family?

11 How is loving your children an extension of loving God?

Prayer

Heavenly Father, grant me rest from my work. Provide and arrange such times that will feed my spirit and quiet my soul before You. Lead me in the way of righteousness. Help me discern the needs of my family and friends and to balance those needs against those of my job and my employer. Lest my work become an idol, I proclaim that You provided my job, and I am willing to move on from it at any time as You direct. Nothing is more important than You, LORD. Teach me to properly prioritize the important areas of my life, neglecting no vital relationship or obligation. When I fail to give appropriate time or weight to anything, please pick up the slack for me and show me how to do better. In all these things, I thank You and trust You. My whole life is in Your hands. As I co-labor with You, I believe You will make it better than I could have imagined. In the name of Jesus, amen.

What will you do to take God to work this week?

Beating Stress and Discovering Joy At Work

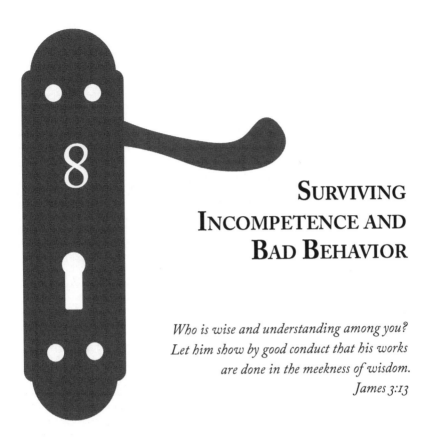

SURVIVING INCOMPETENCE AND BAD BEHAVIOR

Who is wise and understanding among you?
Let him show by good conduct that his works
are done in the meekness of wisdom.
James 3:13

MORE THAN ANY OTHER CHAPTER IN THIS BOOK, this one is about your experience and how to redeem it for God's kingdom on earth. Maybe up to this point in your work life, you thought things just "happened" to you. Good bosses came and went. Bad bosses came and went. Some co-workers became treasured friends. Others drove you up the wall. You may not have seen any rhyme or reason to the parade of people walking through your work life.

From this day forward, we want you to see everyone in your world differently. The people in your work life are a gift from God whom He has entrusted to you so you can make them better—better co-workers, better supervisors, better human beings. You do this not by giving them advice but by exposing them to God's love and care. By showing them how to do every aspect of living in a work family better. By modeling goodness, patience, kindness, diligence, and all the other characteristics of your heavenly Father.

Most Work Problems Are People Problems

Whether your co-workers are as colorful as those I encountered in Chicago during the 1980s, they no doubt pose certain challenges. Unfortunately, some of these co-worker behaviors can damage your career and steal your peace. Given this, we will look at ways to coax colleagues away from bad behaviors and lead them to healthier ways of working together.

The biggest work problems are people problems. In fact, most people change jobs because of relationship issues. However, before running from people problems, it is important to give some thought about whether God has placed that person or group of people in your life for a reason. Difficult circumstances with people can be like sandpaper God uses to smooth out your rough edges and make you more like Jesus.

Just think about the work environment for a moment. Human beings who may have little in common are thrown together, told to work to accomplish one or more goals, and to do it without too many problems. The incentive of continuing to receive a paycheck goes a long way toward motivating people, but it doesn't solve all conflicts. If you are in a place where your co-workers are driving you to distraction, first remember the blessing it is just to have a job. Difficult people, in all their pain and glory, come with the blessing of employment.

Avoid labeling people, because labels can rob them of their freedom to change. The devil is an accuser, but that isn't who you want to align with on life's journey. Your duty is to join the redeeming work of Jesus. Just as the Holy Spirit leads you away from bad behaviors, so you can reinforce healthy behaviors among the people in your office or other workplace.

Nine Cranky Co-worker Behaviors

The following is a list of nine negative co-worker behaviors that may prove to be a challenge to you during your career.

1. The Megaphone

Have you ever had a day, maybe right before a big holiday, when you would rather talk than work? We have all had those kinds of days. But the co-worker who exhibits the megaphone behavior represents something different. He or she has gotten into the bad habit of talking constantly to anyone who will listen. This person's excessive talking drains energy from fellow co-workers who wander into his or her lair. Pity the person who shares a cubicle wall with the constant talker! Gossips come and go from the workstation of the megaphone.

Remedy: Although one person is unlikely to change the megaphone's behavior, you need not get cornered for a long conversation. The first time the megaphone comes up for air, or even before, mention that you have to return to an important task. Then walk away.

2. The Faultfinder

Have you ever met a person who can quickly discern the cloud in every silver lining? One of the least likely people to get promoted in an organization is the one who constantly expresses negative reactions. If you handed this co-worker a bag with one million dollars in it, he or she might reply, "This thing is really heavy." What's worse, this person will tend to find fault with other people, day and night. Like most bad behaviors, finding and expressing the negative side of things is a habit. If you've developed this trait, break it.

Remedy: Help the faultfinders in your organization look at the positive possibilities instead of the inevitable doom ahead.

If criticism comes to mind, ask them to hold onto it until the entire idea is expressed. Then give them an opportunity to turn the potential flaw upside down by suggesting an improvement that fixes the problem and improves the product. This will confirm that they are trying to help—not just being faultfinders.

3. The Volcano

Do you know a co-worker who blows up regularly or with tremendous velocity? This can even be a manager with the patience of a two-year-old. No need to sacrifice yourself (or an unblemished goat) at the hands of this angry tyrant.

Remedy: "A soft answer turns away wrath, but a harsh word stirs up anger" (Proverbs 15:1). Understand that volcanoes need energy to erupt and that it's usually difficult for them to produce that power by themselves. If you refuse to feed into their negative energy cycle, it is possible for them to vent their volcanic personality without you getting burned by their lava.

4. The Bulldozer

It is good to be passionate about your projects. But the bulldozer goes overboard, mowing down anything and anyone that stands between him or her and the completion of the assigned task. Most often, this behavior exhibits itself in a disregard for the importance of everyone else's work. The bulldozer insists co-workers drop everything and help with his or her vital task at hand. No thinking about it . . . just "do as I say."

Remedy: Bulldozers usually cannot be stopped once they have built up a huge head of steam, but they can be slowed down or diverted. If you are genuinely busy with a more important task, let these co-workers know about your priority. Assure them that you will get to their request but ask when they really need it. Give them a realistic timeframe when you can get back to them. Then point them in a direction that does not involve you or your work.

5. The Victim

Have you encountered that co-worker who has trouble getting down to work because conditions are never right? This behavior is all about the perceived pain and suffering of the victim. Bosses like employees who show up, do their work, and find ways to solve their own problems. As President Theodore Roosevelt put it, "Complaining about a problem without proposing a solution is called whining." Noting every microscopic impediment—from the stale candy in the vending machines to the color of the office décor—is not helpful or appreciated. Blaming mistakes on everything and everyone but themselves doesn't promote team unity. The victim's attitude eventually causes resentment in co-workers and frustration in his or her manager. Complaints should be like silver bullets: used annually at most, and less frequently if possible.

Remedy: Help the victims at your work know you found a workaround to whatever problem they name. If their martyrdom is able to stump even you, suggest they do something else productive while they wait for their difficult problem to get fixed.

6. The Snake In the Grass

Beware the co-worker who lies to you or about you! He or she is likely to throw anyone and everyone under the bus to avoid taking responsibility for mistakes. Subversion not only affects the specific employees involved but is also a cancer that eats away at the morale of the whole work unit. Snakes will bite. Once you are sure a person has lied to you, be careful about trusting him or her in the future.

Remedy: If you catch a co-worker in an untruth that negatively affects you, confront him or her with the facts in a non-emotional manner. If the person is spreading untruths about you or your work, make sure to pray before taking action. God may guide you to speak to the employee directly or to provide the alternate set of facts to your supervisor, without specifically accusing your colleague of lying. If you have your facts in order, chances are your boss will figure out what really happened without your accusations against a co-worker. Finally, forgive your co-worker. Building up a resentment against him or her won't help anything.

7. The Microscope

The microscope criticizes even the most minute of details. The truism "pick your battles" seems to be a foreign concept to the person, and his or her nitpicking saps energy and erodes confidence. When co-workers who demonstrate these traits bring up an issue, they do not think about its relative importance to the overall project. Perhaps the microscope in your office is a boss who majors in looking at every detail of a project, second-guessing seemingly inconsequential steps you took to get to the right answer.

Remedy: If you have a boss or co-worker who engages in a high level of scrutiny over the little things, pray for a critical eye in self-editing your own work products. Once you know the level of scrutiny, it is easier to respond with a satisfactory work product. Understand the microscope's importance of attention to detail. Don't allow the urge to finish a task quickly prevent you from going over the finer points with care.

8. The Space Cadet

Everyone forgets tasks, but the space cadet has trouble finding anything on his or her desk. This person has trouble remembering and executing even basic organization skills. Such habitual absentmindedness destroys confidence among his or her co-workers that the job will get done.

Remedy: If you have co-workers who exhibit space cadet tendencies, make a point to follow up with them well before their tasks are due. Help them become better by staying organized enough yourself to help them be on time. Encourage them to write down easily forgotten subtasks and refer to a to-do list often. "Close the loop" on your responsibilities with these teammates by letting them know a task is completed or will be due soon.

9. The Gossiper

The gossiper loves to spread negativity in the workplace. There is an old truism that if a co-worker is talking to you about everyone else in the office, he or she is talking to everyone in the office about you.

Remedy: Shut down gossips by suggesting you go to the person who is the subject of the gossip and ask him or her firsthand about the situation, as suggested in Matthew 18.

Love Your Co-workers Through Their Bad Behavior

As you take time to care about your co-workers and supervisors, even in their bad behavior, you change your own thinking about the situation. Instead of playing the victim, you become partners with God in recreating your work environment. Obviously, your role does not include assuming responsibility for the bad behaviors of others. You can't control those to whom God gave free will, but you know that love makes up for a multitude of sins. The New Testament is full of admonitions to love one another, such as this one: "And above all things have fervent love for one another, for 'love will cover a multitude of sins'" (1 Peter 4:8).

Leaders Are Human Too

If an alien landed a spaceship in your front yard, sci-fi movies suggest his or her early communications would include the well-known phrase, "Take me to your leader." Your reaction may include a cringe and a pained expression. Your temptation might be to suggest the alien talk to someone more genial and wise, like your second-in-command.

"You don't know my boss," you might say sincerely to this being from another world. "Wouldn't you rather meet the assistant manager or maybe my favorite female vocalist?"

"No, really, take me to your leader," the alien would reply with a hint of irritation in his or her almost monotone, electronic voice.

While we are often able to excuse shortcomings (sometimes major ones) in ourselves, we like perfection in our leaders. At work, part of this double standard may stem from the difference in salary. We know the boss gets paid more, so shouldn't he or she be substantially better at everything than us? Or maybe it is an experience issue. After all these years, shouldn't the boss know how to handle a particular situation? After all, the boss has been at it a lot longer than we have...and he or she gets paid the "big bucks."

The truth is few supervisors even approach perfect. They have good days and bad days, just like us. They have strengths, weaknesses, and blind spots. Over the course of twenty years in management, I received a lot of praise from both my employees and bosses. But they criticized me too. Sometimes it was justified, and sometimes not.

The important thing to remember is that bosses *also* have the capacity to change. Just as we shouldn't label co-workers into permanently dysfunctional roles, we shouldn't accuse our bosses of such permanent failings either. Our daily interactions with them will likely make them either better or worse at managing others. The way we respond to leadership, discipline, and advice has the power to transform supervisors from so-so to superior.

Here's one example. Imagine you want to suggest an alternate way of doing something. You can either bring this up humbly and carefully or blurt it out in an accusatory manner. Allowing everyone, but particularly your boss, the room to maintain his or her dignity is important. Never be critical or correct a boss in front of others. Respect is the key. If you frame your ideas as helpful suggestions, you have a much better chance of seeing them enacted.

Even if bosses seem completely incompetent and not up for the challenges of their post, it is not your responsibility to expose them or bring them down. God put them in your life, so learn what you can from them and realize your relationship is only for a season. It won't last forever; either they will go, or you will. Nothing is permanent. Until then, help them the best you can to accomplish the overall mission. Make them look as good as possible. Remember that if the boss looks bad, the entire section or department may be viewed as bad also. It's just like out at sea: if the captain hits an iceberg, everyone on the ship sinks. Helping the boss navigate troubled waters may not only endear you to the captain but also others as well.

Although it is difficult for people to change at their core, you can bring out the best or worst in your supervisors. As another example, imagine you want to address your supervisor's tendencies to micro-manage you. If you calmly explain the problem to your supervisor, he or she might give you a chance to prove you don't need as much oversight. Or your supervisor might suggest you do *A*, *B*, and *C* to put his or her mind at ease, perhaps by copying them on actions at key points in the process. (Let the supervisor see your progress.) On the other hand, if you label the supervisor a micro-manager and don't talk to the person about it, you leave him or her with no room to change. This will put your supervisor in a box and will do nothing to help him or her learn healthier ways of managing.

A supervisor's tendency to helicopter around you may be in response to perceived shortcomings in your game, such as not closing the loop on significant tasks. Do you keep your boss informed (at the level he or she desires) when tasks are completed or delays interfere with deadlines? Some supervisors desire more feedback than others. Figure it out and manage your boss's expectations appropriately. Whether he or she wants constant updates or an occasional check-in, make sure you understand the expectations and adjust your feedback accordingly. This will save you considerable frustration.

Responding to Critical Leaders or Co-workers

Next, let's look at some of the ways to respond when our leaders and co-workers show just how human they can be toward us.

Responding With Kindness

While noticing the faults of others comes naturally, responding in a Christ-like fashion will take practice, patience, and discipline. Looking honestly at our own imperfections will infuse us with the grace we need to extend to others. We must seek to understand the motivations of our leaders, even when they aren't offering us the same courtesy. "Let your speech always be with grace, seasoned with salt, that you may know how you ought to answer each one" (Colossians 4:6). Grace means undeserved favor. We need it from God and we owe it to others.

Responding By Blessing, Not Cursing

Our words are powerful—probably more powerful than we realize—and Scripture warns us to stay positive when it comes to other people. "Bless those who persecute you; bless and do not curse" (Romans 12:14). Based on thirty-three years as a Christian in the workforce, believe me when I say there are all kinds of negative consequences that follow disrespecting your leaders. Just a few include morale plummeting, productivity tanking, and teamwork disappearing. Even if your boss isn't as gracious as the princess in a fairy tale, continue to bless him or her and let God handle the rest.

We shouldn't respond in kind when our boss or co-workers come at us with unfair criticism. "A soft answer turns away wrath, but a harsh word stirs up anger" (Proverbs 15:1). The more we maintain self-control, the more we will come out looking professional when others go low. Even if a boss is downright evil, remember Jesus stepped down from heaven into a world overwhelmed by evil. He fought back by modeling good in every aspect of His life. By responding in a peaceful way, our tone may be transformative for our boss. "Where there is no wood, the fire goes out; and where there is no talebearer, strife ceases" (Proverbs 26:20).

Responding With Humility

Humility is about understanding the depths of our own immaturity. (If we truly knew the limits of our understanding, it would be hard for us to have a prideful attitude.) If God chooses us to help our boss improve, we need to do it with meekness, knowing our wisdom is coming from God and not from within ourselves. No one responds well to anyone with a prideful attitude.

We must strive to keep our own behavior in line with Scripture and our faith. Paul suggested to the Christians in Rome, "Bless those who persecute you; bless and do not curse. Rejoice with those who rejoice, and weep with those who weep. Be of the same mind toward one another. Do not set your mind on high things, but associate with the humble. Do not be wise in your own opinion" (Romans 12:14–16). Generally, we can cover almost any topic with anyone if we state our opinion with meekness and exhibit genuine concern for the person's best interest. "Who is wise and understanding among you? Let him show by good conduct that his works are done in the meekness of wisdom" (James 3:13).

Responding With Forgiveness

The number one arrow in the quiver of the Christian is forgiveness. When we fire a flaming arrow of forgiveness at our enemies, they often melt. Whether it be a co-worker who did us wrong or a supervisor who overlooked us for a promotion, forgiveness defuses all the bad feelings and tension. "Bearing with one another, and forgiving one another, if anyone has a complaint against another; even as Christ forgave you, so you also must do" (Colossians 3:13). Notice Paul doesn't say that because Christ forgave us, we *might* choose to forgive others. We must forgive because hate and its lesser cousins are not acceptable in God's eyes and make for miserable roommates.

Acts Of Goodness

At each stage in our relationship with another person, we have the choice to forgive or not forgive. Whenever we choose unforgiveness, it sets the relationship down the path to deterioration:

  1 Remedy Stage: "Let's fix the problem."
  2 Responsibility Stage: "Who caused the problem?"
  3 Rights Stage: "I'm right, so you must be wrong."
  4 Removal Stage: "Get rid of those people."
  5 Revenge Stage: "Make someone pay."

If we find ourselves in this cycle, it is time for prayer. "You shall not take vengeance, nor bear any grudge against the children of your people, but you shall love your neighbor as yourself: I am the LORD" (Leviticus 19:18). There are two ways we can avert this cycle.

First, *do not be overcome by evil.* Evil compounds evil. When we get defensive and try to fight back, our bosses or co-workers might just escalate the situation. Our fallen human nature whispers "retaliation" in the ear of the aggrieved, but love commands us to overlook the slight and trust God for the answer. As Christians, we don't believe in karma, but we do believe a just Father protects His children unless there is a larger point to be made through our suffering.

King David expressed natural contempt for his enemies, even as he turned his right to retaliate over to the LORD. "As for the head of those who surround me, let the evil of their lips cover them; let burning coals fall upon them; let them be cast into the fire, into deep pits, that they rise not up again" (Psalm 140:9–10).

Second, *overcome evil with good.* Many times, evil can only be overcome with good. Our acts of goodness toward those who mean to harm us will put them in a difficult situation. They must either change their attitude toward us or override their conscience to continue the fight. Our loving gestures toward them becomes a testimony before God. "If your enemy is hungry, give him bread to eat; and if he is thirsty, give him water to drink: for so you will heap coals of fire on his head, and the LORD will reward you" (Proverbs 25:21–22).

David again provides advice on how to do this:

Fierce witnesses rise up; they ask me things that I do not know. They reward me evil for good, to the sorrow of my soul. But as for me, when they were sick, my clothing was sackcloth; I humbled myself with fasting; and my prayer would return to my own heart. I paced about as though he were my friend or brother; I bowed down heavily, as one who mourns for his mother (Psalm 35:11–14).

Angry Fix

There is one approach to definitely avoid when dealing with leaders: *getting angry*. Don't give in to angry fixes for problem behaviors. Losing your cool will seldom solve a situation, and there is great risk to your career and witness when you cede control to unbridled emotions. Instead, focus on the *remedy* to bad behavior and take responsibility for your own side of the street. If you did anything to trigger your co-worker's bad behavior, take note of your actions and pray you learn not to incite the perpetrator. Apologize if appropriate. Don't focus on your rights or the other person's wrongs but on promoting peace in the office. "For the wrath of man does not produce the righteousness of God" (James 1:20).

If you find that your emotions are getting away from you, you may need to remove yourself from the troubling situation and take a break. Give up any feelings of entitlement to revenge. "Repay no one evil for evil. Have regard for good things in the sight of all men. If it is possible, as much as depends on you, live peaceably with all men. Beloved, do not avenge yourselves, but rather give place to wrath; for it is written, 'Vengeance is Mine, I will repay,' says the LORD" (Romans 12:17–19). Trust God to make everything right in the end.

Instead of giving in to angry emotions, give them away. Of course, your best example in this will be Christ.

> For to this you were called, because Christ also suffered for us, leaving us an example, that you should follow His steps: 'Who committed no sin, nor was deceit found in His mouth'; who, when He was reviled, did not revile in return; when He suffered, He did not threaten, but committed Himself to Him who judges righteously (1 Peter 2:21–23).

Some claim that Christ, being part man and part God, had an advantage to us, but He is to be your example in all things. You may not live up to His example, but your charge is to try your best.

Maturing as a Christian means giving up fleshly defense mechanisms in favor of heavenly ones. Due to several unpleasant experiences from my youth, I determined the best defense included a nuclear response to any hurt. If someone said something that intentionally or even unintentionally hurt my feelings, I hit back harder—trying to cut my attacker to the quick. As I've grown in the LORD, this human frailty occasionally tries to slip back into my life. Prayer reminds me, "Bearing with one another, and forgiving one another, if anyone has a complaint against another; even as Christ forgave you, so you also must do" (Colossians 3:13).

Summary

Most work problems are people problems. Although it's important to be task-focused and accomplish our part of the company's mission, our future effectiveness will depend on the relationships we cultivate with co-workers, supervisors, and customers in the workplace. For this reason, we need to understand several problematic co-worker behaviors and the human frailties of our leaders so we can know how to use kindness, blessing, humility, and forgiveness to deal with these people in our work lives. If we have deteriorating relationships at work, acts of goodness may be able to save the day. We must always avoid the angry fix. While an angry response may feel good in the moment, we will pay a price later in addition to grieving God.

Spotlight Feature

Eric Walker

Eric Walker has climbed the ranks from novice to senior professional during the course of his twenty-plus year career in the complex world of information technology. His stops have included government, large government contractors, and smaller information technology firms. His experience with state-of-the-art equipment and knowledge of technology systems has made him a sought-after expert and has led to promotions, awards, and new opportunities.

A devout Christian and native Oklahoman, Eric takes his faith to work and tries to maintain a good witness with his co-workers. Although he is human, he practices his profession with high ethical standards and prides himself on helping his employers do things the right way.

More than once in his career, Eric has encountered serious ethical dilemmas when his supervisors asked him to misclassify equipment costs or mischarge labor to the wrong accounts. In one case, he had to hold the line against substantial pressure to misclassify a $1 million piece of Cisco equipment to replace a failed component, which could not be properly charged to a current contract. Eric's company also asked him to use alternative identification numbers so the part could be inappropriately charged to a government contract.

It didn't take a lot of prayer or Bible study for Eric to know the request was just plain wrong. The situation tested his faith and determination, but he held strong and refused to falsify the information. Eric's moral stand proved unpopular with management. Although he had previously been considered a top performer (receiving excellent performance ratings and awards), he was abruptly labeled "not a team player." Three years later, he became the first person laid off when the company downsized, though at the time he ranked as his team's top performer. Eric didn't argue what seemed like a reprisal for his unwillingness to go along with the improper charging, and God quickly provided another job for him.

One of Eric's major motivators for working is giving to his local church and various Christian causes. He is motivated by Hebrews 7:8, which states, "Here mortal men receive tithes, but there [Jesus] receives them, of whom it is witnessed that he lives." Eric knows that when he gives, he is storing up riches in heaven and helping real people here on earth.

When he gets discouraged after a particularly hard day at work, Eric reminds himself of Jesus' words from Matthew's Gospel:

> Do not lay up for yourselves treasures on earth, where moth and rust destroy and where thieves break in and steal; but lay up for yourselves treasures in heaven, where neither moth nor rust destroys and where thieves do not break in and steal. For where your treasure is, there your heart will be also (Matthew 6:19–21).

Spotlight Questions

What could you identify with in Eric's story?

What action steps occurred to you about taking God to work?

Study Questions

1   *Read Romans 12:18.* What are some bad behaviors you've seen in your workplace?

2   How is it possible to live at peace with your co-workers in spite of their behaviors you find annoying?

3   *Read Romans 12:14–16.* When was a time you had to bless those who cursed you or treated you badly at work?

4   How can kindness overcome evil or make a bad situation better?

5   What does it mean to be high-minded or wise in your own opinion?

6   *Read James 3:13–18.* How does good conduct show that your works are done in "the meekness of wisdom"?

7   In what way would bitter envy and self-seeking cause a person to boast against the truth?

8   How is pride at the root of many workplace disagreements? Give an example.

9   *Read Romans 12:17–19 and 1 Peter 2:21–23.* How can responding in anger make things worse instead of better?

10   How can Jesus' example help you respond correctly to issues in the workplace?

11   What is involved in committing yourself to God during your trials?

12   *Read Psalm 140:9–10 and Proverbs 25:21–22.* How can you keep from being overcome by evil?

13   What are some concrete ways you've overcome evil with good in the workplace?

14   What is one step you can take this week to help a leader or co-worker who exhibits less-than-productive or even destructive behavior?

Prayer

Heavenly Father, thank You for Your most amazing creation: people. Teach me how to love all those You have placed in my life for this season. Show me how to learn from even the most difficult co-workers and bosses while trusting You to mediate our differences. Bring peace to every area of my life as I yield the control to You. Show me how to care for the most unlovable people in my workplace. Teach me to get along with everyone by maintaining a humble spirit, a helpful attitude, and appropriate boundaries when needed. Show me how to overcome evil with good. Mostly, just remind me to come to You when I have difficulties with people. Guide me back to Your loving counsel and wisdom. In the name of Jesus, amen.

What will you do to take God to work this week?

LIVING BEYOND
PAYCHECK TO PAYCHECK

But seek first the kingdom of God and His
righteousness, and all these things
shall be added to you.
Matthew 6:33

CHALMA DIDN'T CONSIDER HERSELF A MODEL EMPLOYEE at the Department of Energy, but she worked hard just the same. She stayed late several occasions each month, and her performance appraisals reflected an above-average aptitude for her position. Her career occupied an important place in her life. So, a call from Jeremy at the Security Office surprised her on what had been a glorious Tuesday morning.

"Is this Chalma Brown?" the gruff voice on the other end asked.

"Yes, it is. How may I help you?"

"We need you to come over to the Security Office today and discuss some issues with us. Are you available at 2:00 PM?"

Chalma looked at her schedule and indicated her availability to come for the meeting at two o'clock. Immediately her mind raced, wondering why security would want to talk to her.

The sun shone bright and the trees sported new light green leaves, apropos for late spring in the District of Columbia. The ride on the shuttle from her building over to the Security Office on the main campus gave her plenty of time to think. Although jittery inside, her outward demeanor stayed cool as a cucumber.

Chalma's mind raced as she sat in the Security Office waiting room. She kept trying to figure out why she had been summoned. Although single, she had not been dating anyone, so that wasn't the issue. She hadn't travelled out of the country since a mission trip with her church a few years earlier to Haiti. Then it dawned on her.

Her hopes sank. When she had been given a government security clearance, she had signed on to regular credit checks and committed to avoiding serious credit issues. Her personal finances had gone steadily downhill during the past two years. She had loaned some money to a family member and never received repayment, and as a result she had gotten seriously behind on her car loan. The car had almost been repossessed. She had since used the opiate of instant gratification to steady her nerves about her financial problems. Ultimately, she had lost track of how much she owed on her many credit cards.

Fortunately, the Security Office gave Chalma sixty days to get her credit scores up to the acceptable level. Although it took extreme measures, she found a way to keep her job through radical plasectomy (cutting up her credit cards), raiding her retirement account, and selling her Lexus automobile. Painful, these accommodations to her situation fixed the problem. As she realized how close she had come to the brink, Chalma turned her financial life around and now has a credit score well above the minimum her organization requires to avoid being a security risk.

Financial Shipwreck

Personal finances wreck many a career. Most places of employment now have standards for their employees about maintaining their financial affairs, even if it's as simple as a prohibition against getting collection calls at work. People make wrong choices. Sometimes these unproductive choices come from a lack of knowledge. Other times, disaster comes from rebelliousness or spiritual blindness or trying to keep up with peers.

There is little excuse today not to know how to conduct our financial affairs. Sound financial education is as close as a computer or public library. For Christians, Dave Ramsey remains the dean of financial education. Many churches across the country teach his courses, including Financial Peace University (see www.daveramsey.com/classes). Ramsey's mentor, the late Larry Burkett, also captured many timeless biblical principles in his writing. Burkett's organization, Crown Financial Ministries, continues this legacy of biblical teaching with many resources and programs (see www.crown.org).

Financial ignorance aside, most of our financial mistakes come within earshot of sound financial advice. We choose short-term wants over long-term security. A vacation sometimes takes a higher priority than aggressively paying down credit cards. Buying a new car takes precedence over making do with a used one. It doesn't have to be that way. We can choose to delay gratification and put financial security ahead of momentary pleasures.

The rise of modern financial management skewed the value proposition of work by separating our work from payment for our efforts. Direct deposit means most of us don't even see our paycheck. If we use automatic bill payment through our bank, we may have only a couple hundred dollars of discretionary spending power each month. The rest is spoken for before the deposit comes into our checking account. Is it any wonder that many young people today fail to embrace the value of working?

Over the years, the purposes behind working have expanded beyond just salary. Most of us expect full-time jobs to provide health insurance, life insurance, and retirement savings matching.

Beyond tangible benefits, people want fulfillment, and most need to understand their work is contributing to the greater good in some way. We all want significance—to make a difference in the world. This latter motivation can be stronger in some people than even the desire to meet their basic needs. How can an accountant derive meaning in keeping track of the construction costs associated with a new superstructure? The answer is only if the accountant can tie his or her actions to the eventual value added by the new high-rise. God intends for His people to grasp this concept. Our work contributes to His care for the world.

What God Values

As Christians, we want to understand how our jobs tie into God's greater mission for mankind. Whether we mow lawns, cut hair, or run a multi-billion-dollar company, our work helps to care for the people God created. This value proposition surpasses the idea of working to make a living or creating worthwhile services or products. To really embrace our calling to work in the secular world, we must understand this view.

We must grab hold of the understanding we are acting as the very hands and feet of God by caring for His world through our work. Our products and services manifest God's care for our fellow human beings. When we involve God in our work, He becomes part of our attempts to bless His world. "Now then, we are ambassadors for Christ, as though God were pleading through us: we implore you on Christ's behalf, be reconciled to God" (2 Corinthians 5:20). The way we do our job should shout, "Be reconciled to God!"

Internalizing our higher calling allows us to work each day as unto God. We see with the eyes of the Holy Spirit though the clutter of our natural existence to the spiritual essence of our eternal life in God's kingdom. Before we depart earth for heaven, our great calling, our eternal work has already begun. Each new day is a fresh opportunity to show God's love through working. Realizing the freedom of willingly participating in this great calling is vital to staying energized throughout a long career.

At an even higher level, something we say or do may cause an eternal effect on someone we meet. As we co-labor with God, we may influence where that person spends eternity and the quality of the rest of his or her life on earth. Our significance becomes mind-blowing as we understand our potential in the hands of God.

Work Ethic

As a pastor, I would be the first to tell you beliefs are both taught and caught. My parents played a critical role in teaching me and my brother about the importance of a strong work ethic. Their example made a deep impression on us. Neither of my parents graduated from high school or earned high salaries. Dad worked at a factory, and Mom worked for the city recreation department. They faithfully went to work day in and day out, year after year. They didn't complain about their bosses or imply their wages were unfair.

Mom and Dad often volunteered for overtime at their jobs. They took God to work, did their jobs to the best of their abilities, and managed their money well. God blessed their work ethic and respect for biblical principles. At home, my brother and I were assigned chores and were expected to perform them without pushing back. Somehow, the way my parents involved us in the work of keeping up our house made us eager to help. Both my brother and I sought part-time jobs in our teens, even though I also played football in high school.

Today, my parents enjoy a nice retirement. Because of their efforts and emphasis on education, my brother became the first one in our family tree (to our knowledge) who graduated from college. Fortunately, I earned a scholarship to play football in college, but my parents still helped with some of my expenses, like clothing and incidentals.

By watching how they conducted their lives, I caught their work ethic and made it my own. My commitment to giving my all at work and at home came from them. I've tried to teach my children the same values, and I'm often proud of their accomplishments as well.

If you are a parent, recognize the important role you play in the lives of your children and how they will or will not take God to work. Talk to them about the spiritual side of working for the glory of God. Show them how they can use work to take care of God's world. Your kids are watching how you work, and it will influence how they live their lives. Your contribution to your children's value system elevates your work life beyond living paycheck to paycheck.

Sound Financial Footing

The Bible talks about money as much as any other subject. Money has been a major source of interest for human beings since its inception. The following are just a few of the key biblical principles regarding money.

1 God owns it all, and we are managers of His resources.

2 Work is essential to supporting ourselves and our families.

3 A tenth of what we receive should be given back to God.

4 The only way to prosper is to spend less than we earn.

5 A borrower is servant to the lender.

6 God will provide for those who are following Him. This provision usually involves work—which He, in turn, will bless.

7 Being content with the earnings from our labor is a gift from God, which comes from experience.

8 Earthly riches don't last and should not be pursued to the detriment of our spiritual health, our families, or our physical health. "Will you set your eyes on that which is not? For riches certainly make themselves wings; they fly away like an eagle toward heaven" (Proverbs 23:5).

How to Escape Living Paycheck to Paycheck

Living paycheck to paycheck means being under constant financial stress and knowing we are only a paycheck away from financial disaster. A CareerBuilder research report released August 24, 2017, revealed that seventy-eight percent of U.S. workers live paycheck to paycheck to make ends meet.[3] As Christians, we need not fall into this trap. However, once we are ensnared, we need to be willing to take the following strong medicine to escape.

Ask For God's Help

If anything deserves prayer, our financial lives need this kind of help. Healthy finances form a foundational stone to almost every productive person's life. Money affects our ability to drive, eat right, live where we feel called, and give to spread the gospel. Sometimes, we hold back this part of our lives because we really don't want God's advice and wisdom. Many of us would rather shop and mindlessly run up our credit cards than stay home and eat beans and rice.

Remember to pray about your financial decisions and your daily ability to live within your means. Repent of past mistakes and seek God's help for the future. "But the end of all things is at hand; therefore be serious and watchful in your prayers" (1 Peter 4:7).

Keep Good Records

One of the tenets of good stewardship is the principle of diligent accounting. We want what we want when we want it. In my own life, many of my financial mistakes stemmed from purposeful ignorance. Stopping to consider the long-term effects can save us from these particularly boneheaded moves. "Be diligent to know the state of your flocks, and attend to your herds; for riches are not forever, nor does a crown endure to all generations" (Proverbs 27:23–24).

A proper accounting sounds complicated, but it isn't. There are four essentials we need to know about our finances: (1) what we owe, (2) what we own, (3) what we earn, and (4) where it goes.

Do Financial Check-ups

Most trips to the financial pit are long and gradual. We tell ourselves fiscal salvation will come down the road somewhere via a job promotion, salary increase, inheritance, selling our home, and the like. The truth is that it is always possible to outspend any salary, windfall, or inheritance, particularly if we start the spending before the increase is received.

The best way to avoid financial doom is to do regular check-ups and get in front of trends that point us in the wrong direction. The prophet Haggai's warning holds true as we consider finances:

> Thus says the LORD of hosts: 'Consider your ways! You have sown much, and bring in little; you eat, but do not have enough; you drink, but you are not filled with drink; you clothe yourselves, but no one is warm; and he who earns wages, earns wages to put into a bag with holes.' Thus says the LORD of hosts: 'Consider your ways!' (Haggai 1:5–7).

Plan Your Spending

The key to controlling spending is budgeting. God wants us to enjoy the fruit of our labors. He takes delight in seeing us earn money and spend it appropriately. He wants to bless us with an abundance and with contentment. "The plans of the diligent lead surely to plenty, but those of everyone who is hasty, surely to poverty" (Proverbs 21:5). If we run out and spend each dollar as we make it, trouble lies ahead. Ignorance plus easy credit are a recipe for disaster.

As a young person, I had the mistaken impression that those who control credit would proactively keep me out of trouble. I thought they consulted reliable tables and charts to understand how much credit I could handle. Whatever they predicted would come to pass in my life, regardless of my behavior. Little did I know that lenders are incentivized to provide credit, not necessarily use good judgment. Car dealers want to sell us a car. They will find clever ways to justify loaning us the required money, even if they know we will have difficulty paying back the loan. The same is true of mortgage lenders, credit card companies, and furniture stores.

For this reason, it is totally up to us to budget and figure out how much we can afford before we make any major purchases. Jesus taught us, "For which of you, intending to build a tower, does not sit down first and count the cost, whether he has enough to finish it—lest, after he has laid the foundation, and is not able to finish, all who see it begin to mock him, saying, 'This man began to build and was not able to finish'?" (Luke 14:28–30). We need both a short-term and long-term plan.

Every Christian should have a budget that includes line items for tithes and giving. A tenth of our earnings belong to God. Beyond that, we give offerings to help those in need, support mission work, and participate in other worthwhile charities. But even this spending needs to be done in a disciplined way.

It is possible to put ourselves in financial peril by giving more than God approves of or to the wrong cause. So we need to pray about it. "Do not withhold good from those to whom it is due, when it is in the power of your hand to do so. Do not say to your neighbor, 'Go, and come back, and tomorrow I will give it,' when you have it with you" (Proverbs 3:27–28).

Give Obediently Back to God

As mentioned elsewhere in this book, God provides everything we receive. Paying tithes shows we understand this and appreciate His provision. Like saving, tithing is a practice that becomes a habit. The first thing we should always do with our income is to give obediently back to God. It is a commandment with promise. "Honor the LORD with your possessions, and with the first-fruits of all your increase; so your barns will be filled with plenty, and your vats will overflow with new wine" (Proverbs 3:9–10).

Tithing produces blessing! By remembering to honor the LORD, we open up the channels of blessing to flow back in our direction. As the prophet Malachi wrote, "'Bring all the tithes into the storehouse, that there may be food in My house, and try Me now in this,' says the LORD of hosts, 'if I will not open for you the windows of heaven and pour out for you such blessing that there will not be room enough to receive it'" (Malachi 3:10).

Act Your Wage

Some people believe feelings and urges are uncontrollable. This is simply not true. All types of feelings knock on our mind's door, but Christians must practice the discipline of weighing the spirits and sending the negative thoughts packing. Contentment is a feeling we can nurture through thankfulness. Stopping to bless each meal and thanking God for our homes each day will help to build contentment within us. We need to take time to be thankful for all God provides in our lives. "Let your conduct be without covetousness; be content with such things as you have. For He Himself has said, 'I will never leave you nor forsake you'" (Hebrews 13:5).

Experiencing pleasure should never be our primary purpose or motivating factor for living. Animals wander the earth looking for their next meal and their next pleasurable experience. Men and women have a higher purpose: to worship God and to serve Him and each other. "He who loves pleasure will be a poor man; he who loves wine and oil will not be rich" (Proverbs 21:17).

Addictions can cost more than just money, but most of them cost plenty. Spending time and energy letting an addiction run us around our town or city, draining our bank account, is not God's best for us. Instead, we need to get help and commit to loving the precious life that God provides to us. "Why do you spend money for what is not bread, and your wages for what does not satisfy?" (Isaiah 55:2).

Getting into debt is the quickest way to bondage. We have to learn how to live within our means and develop a plan to escape the burdens of debt and live free. The short-term pleasure of charging a vacation on our credit card pales in comparison to the pain of not being able to pay for our basic needs or even losing our marriage over long-term debt. "The rich rules over the poor, and the borrower is servant to the lender" (Proverbs 22:7).

Save For the Future

Saving is a habit. If we get accustomed to always living on less than we earn, there will always be a surplus for the lean times. One thing in life is certain, and that's the unexpected. No matter how smoothly things have been going, there will come a day when something different will happen. A booming economy will end and leaner times will start. Declining interest rates will change to rising interest rates. We need to be ready for changing times. "There is desirable treasure, and oil in the dwelling of the wise, but a foolish man squanders it" (Proverbs 21:20).

In addition to saving for our own retirement (be sure to divide retirement savings among multiple investments in case one or two of them don't perform well), there will be times when we will want to help someone in need. This might be our children or other relatives, or it might be a total stranger. "There is one who scatters, yet increases more; and there is one who withholds more than is right, but it leads to poverty. The generous soul will be made rich, and he who waters will also be watered himself" (Proverbs 11:24–25).

Giving to others takes money. Leaving money for our children and loved ones takes discipline. "A good man leaves an inheritance to his children's children" (Proverbs 13:22).

More Than Money

A woman named Rebecca had anger issues at work. As a long-time cashier for a major grocery store chain, she lived in fear of customer complaints and failure to live up to her employer's demands. The pressure of her job was not in her interactions with customers—she actually liked many of them. Rather, her concern involved fear of being unfairly judged during those times when her line didn't move as fast as some of the other cashiers.

At her store, the customers were invited to help bag their groceries if they so desired. Sometimes, several customers in a row would decline or just couldn't physically help with the bagging. Rebecca stayed fastidious about carefully bagging like items together and avoiding combinations that could damage one product or another. Yet even with the care she took, one time a customer complained because she put two onions (surrounded by their own plastic bag) in the same outer bag as a bunch of bananas. This earned Rebecca a talking-to by her manager.

Over the years, the pressure and fear took a toll on Rebecca, and she became discouraged. She needed God to change her attitude and take away her fear and anger. After hearing one of the messages in the *Taking God to Work* series at Capital Baptist Church, she could feel a transformation begin inside her.

On a particularly busy day, her line started slowing down because several customers in a row didn't help with bagging. The person who came along next was an older lady with many items in her basket. She looked frail and obviously wasn't going to do her own bagging. As Rebecca turned to begin bagging the woman's groceries, she heard God speak to her within her spirit. He said, "Rebecca, will you bag these groceries for Me?"

When she happily replied that she would, the years of anger and fear lifted off her shoulders. God set Rebecca free from her fears and put her to work *for Him*, not just for an employer. More than a paycheck, Rebecca began taking care of God's world that day.

Later, she heard the song, "The King of Heaven Wants Me." It solidified her worth, knowing that no matter what others thought of her, God finds her beautiful. Since then, Rebecca has brought a new attitude to her work. Joy has replaced anger and meaning took the place of resentment. Now she does her cashier job with intention, as unto the LORD. She finds it an honor and a privilege to help people for the Master.

Financial Stability

Many people confuse being financially stable with being independently wealthy. Financial stability means bills are paid on time and money is available for a reasonable standard of living. It also usually implies the stable person has an emergency fund (bank account) with three to six months of living expenses safely tucked away. If someone is independently wealthy, it means they don't need to work in the future. Their fortune is sizable enough that their money and/or interest from safe investments will adequately pay their living expenses and reasonable desires for their expected lifespan.

It's easy for the average worker to get confused about these two concepts, throw up his or her hands, and say, "I will never be financially well!" This may be true if you mean financial independence from working. However, almost anyone can eventually become financially stable.

Getting Free From Debt

Many of us have found ourselves deeply in debt at one time or another. Sometimes, this is directly attributable to bad choices we have made (such as spending more than we've earned, burying ourselves in student loans, or risking large amounts of money in shaky investments.) At other times, we may end up in significant debt due to no fault of our own (such as through an illness that causes huge medical bills, a spouse acting deceptively about finances, or tough economic times shuttering our employer).

When the debt level is high, financial stability may seem a long way off. Our subconscious mind may play tricks on us to sabotage plans for getting out of debt and becoming financially stable. However, with God's help and our determination, most can find a way out of debt and into financial stability. The problem is we really don't *want* to feel the pain of financial discipline. By throwing up our hands and saying it's hopeless, we can go out and spend fifty dollars on dinner for two instead of cooking chicken and rice at home for less than ten dollars.

Financial stability is not only a worthy goal but also an amazing accomplishment. Once we feel the security and stability of sustainable financial practices, we won't know how we survived without them. God wants to show us that life is about more than constantly fighting with creditors or letting ourselves down because of broken finances. If we trust Him, He will teach us how to manage our money and find stability.

"The blessing of the LORD makes one rich, and He adds no sorrow with it" (Proverbs 10:22). With determination and God's blessing, we can find financial security.

Summary

Living paycheck to paycheck is all too common today, even though the way we handle our personal finances can greatly impact the trajectory of our careers. If our financial ship is in danger of running aground, it makes sense to revisit the value proposition of work. Are we spending too much or earning too little? It could be a combination of the two. By inviting God into our finances, keeping good records, doing check-ups of our financial condition, and planning our spending, it is possible to pay down debt and eventually increase savings. One of the key concepts is to "act our wage" and not overspend just because others seem to be getting away with it. Obediently giving back to God and saving are key practices that God often rewards with financial blessings.

Spotlight Feature
Ola Kabazzi

Ola Kabazzi, a contractor for a government agency, found herself battling the demands of the Washington, DC, metroplex for the future of her family. She started her day early in the morning and drove to a commuter lot near her home. There, she stood in line for a ride with a total stranger who coveted her personhood enough to drive her into the city. (By finding two extra people, drivers may use high occupancy vehicle lanes in the Virginia suburbs, which are reserved for vehicles with three or more persons. This cuts the driving time for the driver and the riders. The practice is affectionately known as "slugging.")

Once Ola was in downtown Washington, she found her way to the office and put in a full shift. The pressure to perform and keep her customers happy competed with her desire to be at home more for her three children. After retracing her steps in the evening, she arrived home tired but eager to serve her

family. Ola felt she had to work. It seemed the only way for her
to make ends meet for her family.

As Ola's children grew, she became increasingly concerned
about their education and spiritual development. God led her
to a passage of Scripture that convicted her heart: Acts 17:24–27.
Based on these verses, Ola came to believe that God had called
her to her specific town, block, and household. By running all
over the city, she could not minister effectively where God had
placed her for the present time.

Without telling her husband (at first), Ola enrolled the two of
them in a homeschool convention. As the date of the conference
drew near, she finally asked her husband if he would go along.
He agreed to attend but told her up front that he didn't feel
homeschooling fit their family. By the end of the conference,
he had changed his mind. He agreed with Ola that they would
make ends meet somehow based on his salary alone. His agree-
ment had been one of the conditions Ola told God she needed
to make homeschooling possible for their family.

Ola traded her corporate job for the full-time job of taking
care of her family. The pressures of commuting and pleasing
customers segued into hours with her children and helping them
with their studies. Her primary focus became her family and
her children's education and spiritual development. Since that
time, God has met all of her and her family's financial needs
and proven Himself faithful.

Like many homeschoolers, Ola's children attend labs and
other technical classes once a week at a consortium. This gives
them socialization with other students and a wider range of
curriculum. Ola helped out at the consortium for a year, running several of the administrative functions like collecting fees,
paying the teachers, buying supplies, and distributing them to
the instructors.

Although Ola's new life is not devoid of pressures, the many
external stressors have been replaced by internal questions about

how to serve God and her community better. The encouragement of Scripture and other homeschool mentors have been essential to her success. She reminds herself that Ephesians 6:5–9 says she keeps working as unto God and not to please men. Philippians 2:14 reminds her not to grumble or complain. And 1 Thessalonians 5:18 teaches her to give thanks in all things. These passages have elevated Ola and her family far beyond living paycheck to paycheck.

Spotlight Questions

What could you identify with in Ola's story?

What action steps occurred to you about taking God to work?

Study Questions

1   *Read Matthew 6:6.* What does living paycheck to paycheck mean to you?

2   What does this verse recommend doing with financial issues?

3   *Read Proverbs 27:23–24 and Haggai 1:5–7.* Do you perform regular financial check-ups? Do you live by a budget? Explain.

4   Do you know what you owe? What you own? What you earn? Where it goes?

5   *Read Proverbs 3:27–28, 21:3, and Luke 14:28–30.* How can you be diligent about planning?

6   How is your Christian witness tied into your handling of financial affairs?

7   Without naming names, what example comes to mind about a person's financial situation that has impacted his or her work?

8   *Read Proverbs 21:17, 22:7, Isaiah 55:2, and Hebrews 13:5.* How does covetousness drive human behavior?

9   Why is addiction to pleasure a pathway to poverty?

10 In what way is a borrower the servant to the lender?

11 *Read Proverbs 11:24–25, 13:22, 21:20, and Malachi 3:10.* What practices help you save money?

12 What temptations strongly pull at you to squander money?

13 What is God's promise for the tither?

Prayer

Dear Father in heaven, thank You for the resources You provide. Thank You for my salary, my benefits, and the other financial blessings I've received. Thank You for Your guidance, as reflected in the Bible and taught by Christian men and women through books and other resources. Where education or training is needed, help me to learn how to effectively manage my financial affairs. When the issue is self-control, strengthen my resolve to live by a budget and avoid overspending. Teach me to be an effective steward of the resources You've provided by tithing, giving, paying my bills, and sharing resources with the less fortunate. Help me break my addictions to things that have previously inhibited me from living my financial life in a way pleasing to You. Show me how to be a good financial witness of the power of the gospel. Help me to avoid any appearance of financial impropriety, either in my work or in my personal affairs. I give You the glory for all of Your generous blessings. In the name of Jesus, amen.

What will you do to take God to work this week?

WHEN YOUR JOB IS DRIVING YOU CRAZY

Be anxious for nothing, but in everything by prayer and supplication, with thanksgiving, let your requests be made known to God; and the peace of God, which surpasses all understanding, will guard your hearts and minds through Christ Jesus.

Philippians 4:6–7

SARAH, A SUPERVISOR in a mid-size manufacturing company, strived for excellence each day. Her boss, Katie, was a strong leader with the company. She had mentored Sarah for many years, even before Sarah had joined the management team. Yet in spite of Katie's many positive attributes, she could come across as quite cutting and direct. She bullied some of the other managers, though Sarah did not usually draw her ire.

One day, Sarah sat in the conference room, waiting for the manager's weekly staff meeting to begin. Her colleagues filed in and found places around the crowded boardroom table. Gentle chitchat continued until Katie whirled into the room like a human tornado. Her dark brown hair coifed to perfection, Katie's expensive suit betrayed her love of life's finer things.

"Whoever is putting eggs in the microwave has got to stop," she said with disgust. "It stinks out there. If they don't stop it, I'm going to have all the microwaves ripped out of here. It's going to be too bad, so sad."

Sarah twisted her necklace chain and tried not to look nervous. It bothered her that the leader of this large organization raised her voice about something as mundane as microwave smells coming from the kitchenette.

"I want to hear about end-of-quarter numbers from each of you," Katie continued menacingly. "Sarah, we'll start with you."

Sarah nearly swallowed her tongue as she opened the manila folder sitting in front of her place at the table. Although she felt prepared, Katie's aggressive management style had set her on edge. "Boss, production rose six percent over the last quarter and four percent year over year."

"Tell me something I don't know," Katie fired back. "How many more orders do you expect from customers through year end? Come on, people, you need to be in touch with your customers. Don't just spew numbers at me. What do they mean?"

"No problem," Sarah replied. "I have the latest figures right here. New work should be five percent below last year. So, even though we lost one person, we should have plenty of capacity to meet our year-end production goals. The total number of orders is 190."

Although the answer placated her boss and she moved on to the next person, Sarah felt acid climbing into her esophagus. No breakfast and an extra cup of coffee conspired to bring on acid reflux. Sarah tried not to throw up in her mouth. The stress nearly overwhelmed her. Even when she had the right answers, it never seemed to be enough. She simply had to find a new job, and soon.

Processing Workplace Stress

Stress is a major problem for American workers today. According to the American Institute of Stress website:

- Forty-four percent of Americans feel more stress than they did five years ago
- Twenty percent report being under extreme stress
- Seventy-five percent of doctor visits are for stress-related ailments
- Stress increases the risk of heart disease by forty percent and stroke by fifty percent
- Forty-four percent of Americans report losing sleep every night over stress
- Stress costs American industry $300 billion each year[4]

Fear Increases Stress

One of the major roots of stress is fear. *What if we fail? What if the boss loses faith in us? What if we lose our job? What if the next guy gets the promotion instead of us?* Fear represents a lack of faith. If we believe God's Word about His plans for us, there is no rational reason for fear. We can take comfort that nothing can happen to us at work that Jesus can't eventually make right. If we are in God's will, we can survive almost anything. Trouble can and will come into any life, but as Christians we can depend on our LORD to sort it out with us.

It is impossible to escape from the love of God that has taken hold of our lives as believers. Not only is He the "hound of heaven," but He is also the lover of our souls. He always has another job, another way out, or another plan should things fall apart. What's more, He doesn't want us to live in fear and dread. "For God has not given us a spirit of fear, but of power and of love and of a sound mind" (2 Timothy 1:7).

The remedy to a job that is driving us crazy is to grasp onto God's love for us and those around us. Finding that place of comfort in God each day releases us from fear. Like the waiting arms of a loving parent, God's loving care guards our minds from excessive concern about temporal circumstances.

It is also important for us to gain perspective on our situation when our job is driving us crazy. Christians all over the world have found themselves in extremely difficult situations. Persecution, torture, and starvation represent just a few of the things suffered today by Christians somewhere in the world. If those folks can find solace in Scripture in the midst of such troubles, we ought to be able to find the same for our less odious problems.

If we never felt discomfort, we might never seek the Comforter. We can find hope even when we feel like Paul, who wrote, "We are hard-pressed on every side, yet not crushed; we are perplexed, but not in despair; persecuted, but not forsaken; struck down, but not destroyed" (2 Corinthians 4:8–9). God is there to comfort us.

Don't Worry

Parrots are worriers. If you've owned one of these furry friends, you know their small brains are endlessly curious and constantly concerned about potential threats. It is a dichotomy that keeps them fed and alive in their native jungle habitats. They like the familiarity of their cages and homes, but they become bored if left in a small environment for too long. On the other hand, too many new stimuli in their lives can make them agitated and scared.

My favorite pet parrot enjoyed riding around on my shoulder, pirate-style. Bruno could have spent hours just hanging out and doing whatever I did, *unless* I went to the basement. Although it was furnished, the lower level of my home held no comfort for Bruno. Being below ground did not sit well with her, and she froze in position if I started down the basement stairs. (Bruno got her name before she had a DNA test that revealed her sex.) She didn't do her familiar head bobs or looking around. I could feel the tension in her talons as she held onto my shirt tightly.

She felt petrified, no matte r how many times I tried to desensitize her from fear of the basement. At one point or another, she would release her bowels on my shoulder and send us both upstairs—me for a fresh shirt, and her for the safety of her cage.

I can relate to Bruno's fear. As a lifetime acrophobic (a person afraid of high places), merely looking at a skyscraper could cause my brain to go on tilt. I know, it is irrational to be standing safely on the sidewalk outside a tall building and be scared of a bunch of steel and concrete. Going up in a building beyond ten floors or so was not something I wanted to do.

God carefully planted me in Washington, DC, where the height of buildings is restricted to no taller than the Washington Monument (555 feet tall). This restriction kept my fear manageable and taught me to rely on God for those rare occasions when work or other situations (like jury duty) required me to go near the top of one of our city's mini-skyscrapers.

Like a parrot, I tended to hide my anxiety. In the jungle, prey animals do not want their predators to know of their fear when they draw near. So, parrots put on a strong demeanor and try to hide injuries and illnesses until they are near death. In Washington, DC, I thought the same defense mechanism might be in order for my government career. Little did I know that this coping skill would lead me farther from peace and the help I needed from God.

Finding New Life From a Sabbatical

In 2009, just six years short of retirement age (fifty-five), my anxiety grew to a barely manageable level. Panic attacks suddenly became frequent reminders that something felt dramatically wrong with my life. A trip to the emergency room for a faux heart attack and numerous bouts of dizziness made me realize I could no longer hide my condition. I began to wonder about my ability to continue functioning at a high-stress job. Something had to give.

Eventually, through many circumstances and confirmations, God led me to the decision that I needed substantial time away from work. Although it sounded strange to quit a well-paying and secure government job just six years before retirement, I cashed in my 401(k), took myself out of the game, and opted for a life-saving sabbatical. During the next five months, I renewed my close relationship with God, and He taught me many things about myself and life. The experience became so fulfilling that I wrote a book about it titled *Sabbatical of the Mind: The Journey from Anxiety to Peace*. In the book, I explain how God led me to analyze those parts of my life that caused fear, unhappiness, and disappointment.

God showed me how to find healing from anxiety and more meaning in everyday life. Frankly, I doubt I could have learned so much or changed in so many ways without taking extended time to be alone (mostly) with God. His Word, as revealed in the Bible, and His wisdom, as explained by other godly Christian writers, saved me from the mental turmoil that had robbed me of my peace. After the sabbatical, I returned to my role as a government manager and worked another five-and-a-half year stretch until retirement.

There are times in life when the cumulative burden of stress overcomes us. Work, family obligations, church duties, and other responsibilities have crowded out rest time for so long that taking just one day off fails to soothe us. Even a short vacation may not be enough to reset our mental clock. In such times, God may be calling us—like He did me—to come away with Him for a more extended season of rest and focusing on Him.

A sabbatical implies *active* resting. It isn't just laying around napping in the sunroom (though I did some of that). During my time off, I read dozens of books, improved my physical conditioning, looked up old friends to have lunch, prayed for long periods, and just basked in the presence of God. During this quiet season, God's Word, the Bible, gave me new insights into my phobia and other fears. I came to realize that at the heart of my anxiety lay a failure to apply faith to the immediate concerns around me. Truth be told, we all face fears of some sort. But if deep inside we know our next stop is heaven, there isn't much to fear—even in death.

Due to finances or other pressures, not everyone can take extended time off work. But that doesn't have to prevent you from reserving periods of time to focus on your relationship with God. Whether it be alone time or a Christian retreat or a conference, you can spend a few moments to take the focus off mundane daily tasks and put the focus on your heavenly Father. He wants to communicate with His people and show you just how much He loves you. It's a jungle out there!

Four Steps to Exchanging Stress For God's Peace
1. Trust God Completely
"Be anxious for nothing, but in everything by prayer and supplication, with thanksgiving, let your requests be made known to God" (Philippians 4:6). Stress is carrying a burden that God never intended for you to bear. As previously noted, the root cause of most stress is a lack of faith. If we completely trusted God, there would be nothing to fear or feel stressed out about! Jesus gave the following advice:

> And which of you by worrying can add one cubit to his stature? If you then are not able to do the least, why are you anxious for the rest? Consider the lilies, how they grow: they neither toil nor spin; and yet I say to you, even Solomon in all his glory was not arrayed like one of these. If then God so clothes the grass, which today is in the field and tomorrow is thrown into the oven, how much more will He clothe you, O you of little faith? (Luke 12:25–28).

The Giver of all wisdom is ready, willing, and able to provide you with the answers to your problems. When anxiety begins to creep into your daily life, the words of James 1:5 can help. My rough paraphrase: If you need answers, you can ask God, who is eager to tell you. Once you know the answer, you can ask for anything you need without doubting. Doubting won't get you anywhere with God or in life.

An endless fountain of peace is available to you as a believer. You just have to figure out how to tap into it. "You will keep him in perfect peace, whose mind is stayed on You, because he trusts in You. Trust in the LORD forever, for in YAH, the LORD, is everlasting strength" (Isaiah 26:3–4). The key to finding an overcoming faith is to keep your mind and heart on the Prince of Peace. Consciously find ways to keep God at the forefront of your day, whether that means reading bits of Scripture on cards placed strategically in your desk or listening to a Christian radio station playing in your ear.

There are many other tangible ways that you can practice the presence of God in your workday. Pulling the promises of God into your consciousness will bring transformational change to your mind. "For whatever is born of God overcomes the world. And this is the victory that has overcome the world—our faith" (1 John 5:4).

2. Pray Continually

"Pray without ceasing" (1 Thessalonians 5:17). Prayer is a mighty weapon in the fight against anxiety. But it needs to be a way of life—not just an emergency call for help once our panic is triggered. When stress pushes us to our knees, we are in the perfect position to pray.

The psalmist wrote, "Cast your burden on the LORD, and He shall sustain you" (Psalm 55:22). Take time before the day begins to talk things over with God. Commit your agenda, your meetings, your work products, and your communications to the LORD. Ask for His help to do everything with excellence and in peace.

Once you are in the middle of the fight of life, it's not too late to call on the LORD. He cares about you and wants to help. "Casting all your care upon Him, for He cares for you" (1 Peter 5:7). There is no problem too big for God's power or too small for His concern.

Pray specifically about everything with thanksgiving. You are loved children, and you don't need to slink around and be afraid of God. "Let us therefore come boldly to the throne of grace, that we may obtain mercy and find grace to help in time of need" (Hebrews 4:16)

Remember to be patient in prayer. Sometimes, the answer won't be immediate. Hang in there and keep praying and believing. At some point, change over from requesting answers to just thanking God for what He has already provided and the answers that are on the way. Even if you don't know it yet, God will send a fix to your problem. "Continue earnestly in prayer, being vigilant in it with thanksgiving" (Colossians 4:2).

3. Adjust Your Thinking

Stinking thinking leads to stressful living. Have you ever gotten into such a funk that you can almost smell the bad fragrance of your thoughts? The Christian life is not one mountaintop experience after another, but neither should it include prolonged periods of anger, crabbiness, and unforgiveness. Paul teaches that you can decide what thoughts you allow to hang around in your mind. "Finally, brethren, whatever things are true, whatever things are noble, whatever things are just, whatever things are pure, whatever things are lovely, whatever things are of good report, if there is any virtue and if there is anything praiseworthy—meditate on these things" (Philippians 4:8).

Your thought life matters to God, and it greatly affects changes to your mood. "For as he thinks in his heart, so is he" (Proverbs 23:7). Your daily life is governed by the thoughts you allow to dominate your mind. In just one day, thousands of thoughts may rumble through your brain, but the key is to ponder the good stuff and cast out the bad. You—the real you, the inner person of the heart to which Scripture refers—is different from your mind and should be the boss of your entire being. Your regenerated soul needs to be the gatekeeper over your thoughts and only allow things that are good to remain there. This is the key to letting the Holy Spirit control your life and bring you consistent peace of mind.

If specific thoughts are troubling you, bring them to the foot of the cross and leave them there. If the thoughts insist on coming back, cast them away using Scripture. "Casting down arguments and every high thing that exalts itself against the knowledge of God, bringing every thought into captivity to the obedience of Christ" (2 Corinthians 10:5). As a Christian, you do not have to live in a cesspool of unredeemed thoughts at work or anywhere else.

Let's go back to Philippians and look at the approved list again. These are tried-and-true standards to protect your thought life:

- Is it true?
- Is it honest?
- Is it just?
- Is it pure?
- Is it lovely?
- Is it of a good report (something positive and uplifting)?

Don't be just like everyone else at your office or workplace. Embrace a redeemed attitude about life and be a light to co-workers and managers alike. "And do not be conformed to this world, but be transformed by the renewing of your mind, that you may prove what is that good and acceptable and perfect will of God" (Romans 12:2).

4. Obey Constantly

At some point, your thoughts and prayers need to move you to physical action. Don't just *hear* but *do* the Word of God by putting into practice what you've read in the Bible, heard preached on Sundays, and believed during prayer times. "The things which you learned and received and heard and saw in me, these do, and the God of peace will be with you" (Philippians 4:9).

Do the right thing and you will feel the right way. Peace follows right actions. Disobedience produces stress. It will make you feel out of sorts and cause you to question yourself. If you have gotten into the habit of taking inappropriate or improper shortcuts at work, turn over a new leaf with the help of the Holy Spirit. Ask God to help you change and become a person you can respect again. "Good understanding gains favor, but the way of the unfaithful is hard" (Proverbs 13:15). Don't make your way difficult by doing sketchy things.

Obedience produces peace. Habitually doing what is right will eliminate the need for guilt and disappointment in yourself. Twelve step programs have a motto: "Do the Next Right Thing." When life feels too complicated, there is almost always a "next right thing" to do, even if it's just the laundry. By following God's Word and taking care of life's chores, things usually get better—though it may take time to work through the wreckage of your past.

This will be true of your work life *and* your home life. Trust Jesus and His process for getting you to heaven and help a bunch of people along the way. "Therefore, having been justified by faith, we have peace with God through our Lord Jesus Christ" (Romans 5:1).

Women and Stress

Men and women experience many of the same stressors in the workplace. A demanding boss, inadequate personnel resources, and market changes affect everyone. However, as women continue to expand their presence in the workforce, studies are being done about the ways in which the genders process stress and to what extent it matters.

According to a U.S. government website, "Women often cope with stress in different ways than men. Women 'tend and befriend,' taking care of those closest to them, but also drawing support from friends and family. Men are more likely to have the 'fight or flight' response. They cope by 'escaping' into a relaxing activity or other distraction."[5] The website suggests several tips that can help women (and men) reduce stress:

- *Develop a new attitude.* Become a problem solver, be flexible, get organized, and set limits.
- *Relax.* Take deep breaths, stretch, massage tense muscles, and take time to do something you want to do.
- *Take care of your body.* Get enough sleep, eat right, get moving, and don't deal with stress in unhealthy ways (such as drinking too much alcohol, using drugs, smoking, or overeating).
- *Connect with others.* Share your stress by talking with friends or family, get help from a professional, and help others.

The Cleveland Clinic urges women to slow down long enough to think about how the negative effects of stress might be affecting them.[6] According to the website, women either choose or are forced to take on multiple roles at home, caring for children and parents in addition to work. Stress can lead women to work harder and reach higher in their careers, but it can also cause health problems if not dealt with properly. The bottom line is that women need to focus on stress management activities such as exercise, expressing themselves, keeping a positive outlook, participating in loving relationships, and finding purpose in their lives.

God's Correction

Sometimes our craziness at work or in life is not everyone else's fault. There are times when our behavior contributes greatly to our rough circumstances. God may be allowing some of our chickens to come home to roost to teach us how to live better. God may allow challenges into our lives with the express purpose of helping us grow and change.

In my early twenties, I viewed myself as quite the comedian. Laughter is great, but my way of expressing humor sometimes wandered into disrespecting those I cared about the most. One time at the Christian fellowship I attended, a beautiful young German lady caught my eye. For some reason, she was willing to date me. Although she had my utmost respect, I found myself clowning around with her too often. Eventually, she pulled me aside and asked if I had lost respect for her.

The speech she gave cut me to the quick. When she first met me, I had invited her to my scruffy college house and made her a pretty good lasagna dinner. My manners and willingness to wait on her had won her heart. But in a matter of weeks, I had managed to undo all that work by poking fun at her rigid nature and several other things she held dear. Although our relationship ended with a whimper, I learned a couple of important lessons. People could love the real me without me putting on a comedy show to win them over.

Although it may sting for a moment, God's correction means we are His children. "My son, do not despise the chastening of the LORD, nor be discouraged when you are rebuked by Him; for whom the LORD loves He chastens, and scourges every son whom He receives" (Hebrews 12:5–6). When we find ourselves in a tough situation of our own making at work, we can call on the LORD. He will help us, even when we must suffer a rebuke.

Finding Peace In All Circumstances

At one time or another, your job will drive you at least a little bit crazy. Whether it's the people, the work, the working conditions, the deadlines, or other external factors, circumstances can threaten your inner tranquility. Learning to hold on to the Word of God during such moments will give you great peace.

When your job is driving you crazy, the LORD will provide just the right comfort through a Scripture, a prayer, or a spiritual song—if you give Him the time to do so. "Great peace have

those who love Your law, and nothing causes them to stumble"
(Psalm 119:165). Memorize this or another Scripture to help
you hold on to peace of mind when difficult moments pop up.

Crises will tend to draw you back into God's Word. So, if
your world is going a little crazy just now, make sure to spend
time in your Bible. The solid rock of Jesus is available to you
through God's Word. It gives you something strong to hold on
to when the wind seems to be blowing everything else around.

One of the biggest gifts Jesus left behind on earth is peace. It
became His parting gift as He ascended into heaven following
His resurrection. "Peace I leave with you, my peace I give to
you; not as the world gives do I give to you. Let not your heart
be troubled, neither let it be afraid" (John 14:27). Pursue it and
grab hold of it.

Maybe It's Your Industry

Sometimes, you may find yourself in an industry to which you
are ill suited. If you've held several jobs in your field and are
continually finding yourself miserable, it could be that you are
in the wrong field.

For example, if you are person who hates conflict, jobs that
require negotiation will not be your best fit. If you are person
who loves adventure, accounting won't be the right industry for
you. If you like constantly exploring and learning new things, a
highly routine job will not be one in which you will excel.

As stated elsewhere in this book, all discomfort in a job does
not mean it is time to jump ship. Realize that certain lines of
work invite unethical persons more than others. God may have
planted you in a difficult industry precisely because you live by
His principles. Just realize the baggage that may come with
your journey.

What Are You Thinking About?

The key to having peace in your mind is to guard your thought
life. If your job or any other part of your life is driving you crazy,

the problem usually rests not with other people, places, or things but in your own mind. If you find yourself with such a "thinking problem," the cure is quite simple. Think about something else.

Do you find yourself focusing on the co-worker who doesn't seem to be pulling his or her weight? Replace the negativity, fear, and bitterness with better thoughts, as defined in Philippians 4:8–9. The battle is in the mind. The secret is swapping out negative thoughts, talk, and actions with positive thoughts, talk, and actions.

So instead of going on and on with a lunch buddy about how horrible the other political party is acting, discuss what God is doing in your life. Instead of focusing on what you see as a bonehead move by management, think about how you can boost productivity in your business unit. Instead of complaining about how much work must get done by the end of the day, thank God for your job and praise Him for helping you complete the work by quitting time.

Summary

There are times in our lives when our job will drive us crazy. Stress plays a major part in our lives, which is a problem because it leads to all kinds of diseases that can diminish our effectiveness and shorten our life expectancy. Fear and worry are two of the big drivers behind stress. We need to follow Paul's advice and "be anxious for nothing, but in everything by prayer and supplication, with thanksgiving, let your requests be made known to God; and the peace of God, which surpasses all understanding, will guard your hearts and minds through Christ Jesus" (Philippians 4:6–7).

Depending on how stressed out we become, an extended break may be required. In my book *Sabbatical of the Mind: The Journey from Anxiety to Peace,* I recount my battles with stress and anxiety in the Washington rat race. My sabbatical journey, and the lessons I learned through it, provide a blueprint for coming back from stress. This includes four important steps to peace that could prove the antidote to our job insanity: (1) trust God completely, (2) pray continually, (3) adjust our thinking, and (4) obey to the best of our ability. Philippians 4:8–9 gives us things to think about instead of what is stressing us out.

Spotlight Feature

Pam Nicholson

"Lord, help me," Pam Nicholson lamented one day. "These millennials are driving me crazy." Sitting at her desk in the modern office building, she could hear another person down the hall calling her name. Instead of getting up and walking to her desk, several of her young co-workers preferred to holler down the hall and hope Pam would come to them. While Pam doesn't mind helping, the generation gap often has her at wits' end. Why would her co-workers expect someone three times their age to get up and walk to where they were sitting? "It's not only disrespectful, but lazy," Pam reminds God in an often-repeated prayer.

Although her official title is director of nursing, many in the office call on Pam as the voice of experience. Unfortunately, the demands of her own position keep her plenty busy training and supervising home health aides, who are then assigned to clients across northern Virginia. The company Pam works for was founded by immigrants from Ghana, and many of the employees either immigrated from there or are related to someone from that country. While she applauds the heart behind the company's mission, there is often a language barrier between not only her and the new recruits but also between her clients and some of the home health aides. This is just one of many problems Pam must sort out as she works to match the aides with clients.

Pam enjoys doing intake with new customers. She travels to their homes, often in a place like Warrenton, Virginia, a distant suburb of Washington, DC. Pam determines exactly what is needed for the patient's care. While her firm is not permitted under law to provide medical nursing services, she is a registered nurse and served for many years in emergency room care in Brooklyn, New York.

Pam believes her work is an extension of God's care for her clients. She decides which services the client will need and then assigns a home health aide who might help with bathing, feeding, or other essential needs of the homebound or differently abled. After placing one of her staff in the home, she keeps tabs on the service provided and intervenes if any issues develop. By working with the clients and her staff, she seeks to provide quality care within the parameters of the social or private insurance covering the clients.

Part of Pam's role is to mediate when things aren't going well between a home health aide and a client. "I tell the clients these relationships are like shoes," she says. "If they don't fit, I have more waiting. Matching the right clients and aides is important." Having been in and around nursing for forty-three years, she takes great pleasure in making sure everyone has a smile on their face. If clients are feeling bad, she prays for them and does her best to improve their situation. "If I can leave someone with a smile on their face," she says, "I've been successful."

Nursing of any kind is challenging—both physically, mentally, and spiritually. Although Pam is glad the twelve-hour shifts at the hospital are behind her, she uses her faith every day to deal with troublesome people and difficult circumstances. "Some of the clients we provide services for are very poor," she says. "They need everything. I often end up praying for God's wisdom in how to help." More than anything else, she wants to make sure everyone is satisfied with the services they are receiving. "It really is God's work."

Spotlight Questions

What could you identify with in Pam's story?

What action does Pam's story suggest for you?

Study Questions

1. *Read Philippians 4:6–9.* What makes you anxious in your job?

2. How can prayer help relieve the stress you are feeling?

3. What is the value of adding thanksgiving to prayer?

4. *Read Luke 12:25–28.* What does Jesus say about worrying?

5. What is the relationship between stress and faith?

6. *Read James 1:5.* How can God's willingness to give you wisdom bring comfort from anxiety?

7. *Read 1 Thessalonians 5:17.* How often should you pray?

8. *Read 1 Peter 5:7.* It is a fact that God loves you. How does this verse encourage you to activate His concern for others?

9. *Read Proverbs 23:7 and 2 Corinthians 10:5.* Why is it important to manage your self-talk?

10. What should you do if negative, unhelpful thoughts come to mind?

11. *Read Proverbs 13:15 and Romans 5:1.* If disobedience causes stress, how can you avoid stress?

12. Your justification is by faith. How can the works—which demonstrate your faith—bring peace into your situations at work?

Prayer

Dear Father, I sometimes find my job difficult. Whether it be the people, the tasks, or the situations, my employment wears me down on occasion. Honestly, it makes me feel like I can't endure it for much longer. But You, Lord, are like a fountain of refreshing water. Your Spirit cleanses and refreshes me. Restore to me the joy of my salvation. Help me to live out Your desire for me not to fear but to have power, strength, and a sound mind that I might serve You. Teach me to rest properly when I'm weary. Show me how to commit my days to You and to invite You into every workplace situation. And for all these things, I will thank You and praise You. You are my strength and my joy. In the name of Jesus, amen.

What will you do to take God to work this week?

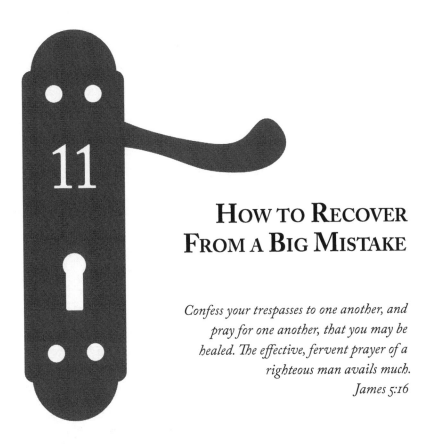

HOW TO RECOVER FROM A BIG MISTAKE

Confess your trespasses to one another, and pray for one another, that you may be healed. The effective, fervent prayer of a righteous man avails much.

James 5:16

ON A COOL NOVEMBER DAY IN 1984, I prepared for another day at my desk job at Tinker Air Force Base, located near Oklahoma City. Little did I know the pandemonium that lurked ahead.

Building 3001 on the base could only be described as behemoth. It served as a repair hangar for large, military jet aircraft and as an office building for hundreds of civilian employees.[7] Throughout the acres of shop area were different types of solvents and other flammable compounds, used by workers to strip paint, repair, and repaint aircraft.

On that day a small-business contractor, working to repair a pipe on the roof, ignited the insulation around a pipe and set fire to the tar-sealed roof. The welder went to get help, and the first firefighter arrived and began dousing the roof with an extinguisher. The blaze temporarily went out but reignited twice more.

Within minutes, it became clear the fire had penetrated the exterior roof and now grew inside a cavity separating the ceiling of the work areas and the roof itself. Soon the firefighters began roaring in, sirens screaming, from every nearby town and city. They headed into the building, and I and many others were evacuated.

It took forty-nine hours and fifteen million gallons of water to extinguish the fire completely. All told, the inferno damaged more than seventeen acres of roof. Area hospitals treated 115 firefighters for smoke-related illnesses during and after the fire. Regular business office employees like myself had several days off with pay as the firefighters worked to extinguish the fire and air out the noxious fumes.

The welder's mistake cost $154 million and took six months of work to repair. While contractors are required to be bonded for such work, the bond is usually no more than a couple of million dollars. In the end, the taxpayers paid for the error.

Fortunately, most of our mistakes are not as large or costly as the Tinker Air Force Base fire of 1984. But none of us are immune to miscues. In this chapter, we will look at errors.

Getting Personal About Mistakes

One of my first significant mistakes involved meeting my new co-workers in a small office on my first day of work at the Chicago Office of Naval Research. The administrative officer walked me around to make introductions. I proudly smiled and shook hands with each of the fifteen or so Navy employees. Most acted quite friendly, but others gave me the oddest stares and even seemed reluctant to shake my hand. I didn't expect an "ahoy there, matey," but the arms-length treatment made me wonder.

I tried to decipher the mixed signals as I returned to my desk. Moments later, I was horrified to find the zipper on my pants had been in the down position the whole time. Not a little bit down, but *all* the way down. Talk about making a first impression! Thankfully, I sported clean boxer shorts for the occasion. Later, one of my co-workers, once he knew me better, remarked that I had seemed "quite open and friendly" at that first meeting.

Historically Momentous Mistakes

Mistakes are a story as old as time. Adam and Eve certainly made a sizable blunder when they allowed sin into their lives and doomed the rest of humanity to living in a fallen world. (In their defense, any one of us would have likely made the same mistake.) And what about the crew of the Titanic not bringing enough lifeboats for all the passengers because builders deemed it unsinkable?

We all make mistakes, but some missteps are definitely bigger than others. The good news is that none of them are too big for God to forgive. The bad news is that sometimes our slip-ups harm others. Making amends might require more than simply expressing regret at the error. Here are a few more of history's greatest mistakes, where a simple "I'm sorry" would definitely not adequately fix the situation:

- Construction of the Tower of Pisa, which began to lean due to being built on an inadequate foundation.
- Decca Records Company turning down the Beatles, because they labeled the music "unsellable."
- Napoleon invading Russia during the winter.
- Russia selling Alaska to the United States for two cents an acre.
- Japan attacking Pearl Harbor with no U.S. aircraft carriers in port (the damage would have been much greater to the U.S. fleet had the Japanese eliminated even one aircraft carrier).

Next, we will look at how to recover from some more common errors.

Mistakes Affecting Only Our Own Work

Everyone makes mistakes in day-to-day tasks. We all forget to do small tasks or omit key data in reports from time to time. Many times, you will discover the snafu before it goes out and be able to fix it. No one finds out about the problem, and it doesn't affect anyone. In those cases, there is no harm done, and you need not bring it up to anyone else.

But what if the flub causes you to lose days or even weeks in accomplishing a project? At some point, this type of error grows beyond the category of affecting only your own work. The right move is to confess your mistake to those affected, offer to jump into fixing the problem, and pray for grace from your employer.

Mistakes Affecting Our Co-Workers

Some misadventures will affect your co-workers. If, after providing input to someone else, you find a submission contains an error, the right thing to do is notify those involved. Timing matters. If the mistake does not immediately affect a task the other co-workers are doing, it's best to get the correct information first and then tell them you need to provide an amended work product. If the project is urgent and there is the possibility they could pass the faulty information up the chain of command or use it to make an immediate decision, you probably should immediately notify all those affected.

Never is quality more important than when fixing an error. Making errors on top of errors will dramatically erode your credibility and be doubly damaging to your reputation. There is nothing funny about a comedy of errors. Before submitting a fix, make sure you have double-checked the correction, whether that means going back to source material, proofreading a revised document from the beginning, or getting a second set of eyes to help you ensure quality.

The hallmark of the Christian worker should be humility and a willingness to accept the consequences for his or her mistakes. Praying for God's help to eliminate mistakes and obtain mercy from our bosses and co-workers should be part of our recovery process.

Mistakes Significantly Affecting Our Employer

Sometimes, blunders significantly affect our bosses or the company as a whole. For example, let's say the information technology lead provides a set of metrics to the CEO of the company. Two weeks later, she discovers inaccurate data caused a key metric to be reported incorrectly. Her bogus data could lead to significant business decisions being made incorrectly—if she doesn't quickly fix the metric and report the mistake.

Although it may cost her job, she must discern how the mistake happened, correct the underlying data, put safeguards in place to prevent a recurrence, and report the revised data to the CEO. Most wise leaders want their employees to feel free to correct mistakes, particularly when the data is heavily relied upon for business planning. Even if this company's CEO didn't respond by giving her another chance, she would have done the right thing.

People-pleasers are those who would rather look good to others than do the right thing. Our purpose first and foremost should be to please God. In his letter to the Galatians, Paul asked, "For do I now persuade men, or God? Or do I seek to please men? For if I still pleased men, I would not be a bondservant of Christ" (Galatians 1:10). It's all about being self-centered or Christ-centered. The life of a Jesus-follower is one that puts others first—even ahead of his or her own reputation.

Mistakes That Cost Us Our Job

People lose their jobs for many reasons that have nothing to do with poor performance or inappropriate conduct. Companies go out of business all the time, and many people lose their jobs as a result. However, in this case, we are talking about blunders that lead to your own job loss. What should you do when your failure costs you your job?

- First, take the failure to God in prayer and ask Him what to do next. Remember He isn't surprised or taken aback. He will no doubt throw in a few lessons to be learned. Ask Him up front what you can learn from the whole situation.

- Understand why you failed. Go deeper than the official reason provided in your termination. Get to the bottom of what factors set you up to fail and figure out how to avoid making the same mistake in the future. If needed, get help from mature Christian friends or a counselor who can help you sort out what happened.

- Recover from the loss. Whether or not your mistake warranted the dismissal, it represents a loss in your life. Pause and regroup. Don't be too hard on yourself. Don't get stuck in hating the personalities and events of the past.

- Based on your understanding of why you failed and what you learned while recovering from the loss, apply for new work that meets your needs, offers you opportunities to serve others, and gets you back in the game of life.

There are situations where the punishment, including job loss, greatly exceeds the magnitude of the transgression. Put simply, you may have gotten fired for a minor offense. In such cases, the organization may have had a different reason for firing you, such as a desire to downsize higher-paid employees to cut costs or to reshape the skill set of their workforce. Whatever the reason, you are still out of the job and need to bounce back. All you can do is analyze what you might have done better. Learn from the situation and seek God for the next steps.

Mistake Versus Failure

If sin is willful wrongdoing, then what is the definition of mistake? I prefer to think of mistakes as either willfully or accidentally doing the wrong thing. Turning down the wrong road might be a driving mistake that costs us an extra fifteen minutes of travel time. We didn't intend to go the wrong way, but we did it without understanding the facts. A mistake becomes sin when we willfully do what we know to be wrong. For example, taking someone else's possessions without their consent is sin.

The primary aggrieved party for sin is always God. When we know our actions fall into the sin category, our first stop in fixing the mistake should be to repent before God. King David of the Old Testament provided a great model of this kind of repentance when he said:

> Have mercy upon me, O God, according to Your lovingkindness; according to the multitude of Your tender mercies, blot out my transgressions. Wash me thoroughly from my iniquity, and cleanse me from my sin. For I acknowledge my transgressions, and my sin is always before me. Against You, You only, have I sinned, and done this evil in Your sight (Psalm 51:1–4).

Obviously, some sins go beyond just offending God. Our willful wrongdoing can cause great harm to others that isn't easily undone. In those cases, we need to own our errors and try our best to make them right. We need to allow God to lead us to the correct actions to fix the problems. By committing ourselves to restitution, we will eliminate cheap grace and focus on undoing the wrong to the greatest extent possible.

How to Recover From Moral Failure

There are times when our mistakes are specific moral failures. We recognize our sin and realize the only path is repentance and cleansing from the LORD. The following is a roadmap for overcoming failure.

Keep Trusting God

The first step to maintaining our trust in God is to recognize His goodness. Although He doesn't condone or uphold us in our sin, He is merciful and loving. He provides for us, often in spite of our waywardness. The book of Isaiah put it this way: "I will mention the lovingkindnesses of the LORD and the praises of the LORD, according to all that the LORD has bestowed on us, and the great goodness toward the house of Israel, which He has bestowed on them according to His mercies, according to the multitude of His lovingkindnesses" (Isaiah 63:7). Remember the loving nature of God. It is the very essence of who He is— "for God is love" (1 John 4:8).

Keep Loving God

We demonstrate our love for God by keeping His commandments. Talking is one thing but doing is another thing entirely. The Gospels repeat this theme throughout. "Jesus said to him, 'You shall love the LORD your God with all your heart, with all your soul, and with all your mind.' This is the first and great commandment" (Matthew 22:37–38).

Our Great Teacher went on to explain how we prove our love. "If you love Me, keep My commandments" (John 14:15). Part of this love relationship includes God's willingness to use our failures to correct our sins. Like a good parent, God is more than the provider of treats whenever we want them. David wrote, "It is good for me that I have been afflicted, that I may learn your statutes" (Psalm 119:71).

Keep Imitating God

Following Jesus is not one long, futile attempt to abide by a list of rules and regulations. Our walk with the Master is about learning His ways and imitating Him. "As you therefore have received Christ Jesus the LORD, so walk in Him" (Colossians 2:6). A big part of avoiding moral failure is to learn how to appropriate God's power in our lives. We can overcome our lesser nature by yielding to God as He crucifies our fleshly appetites. In other words, we don't fight the good work He is doing in us.

As we imitate Christ by following Him, it will have a transforming effect on us. Paul writes about this in his second letter to the Corinthians: "But we all, with unveiled face, beholding as in a mirror the glory of the LORD, are being transformed into the same image from glory to glory, just as by the Spirit of the LORD" (2 Corinthians 3:18). While we don't see God's nature face to face in this life, the glimpses we receive from Scripture, through nature, and through the actions of fellow believers let us know that God is worthy to be followed.

Being transformed into "little Christs," or Christians, includes suffering through the crucifixion of our sinful nature. It can be painful to go through the cleansing of our moral failures, especially as we realize the depth of our depravity and how we have fallen short of God's best for us. Looking to Christ and all He suffered for our sins can bring us into fellowship with Him as we are cleansed. Paul wrote, "I also count all things loss…that I may know Him and the power of His resurrection, and the fellowship of His sufferings, being conformed to His death" (Philippians 3:8, 10).

Failures That Cost Us Our Witness

Sometimes our mistakes cost us not only our job but also our Christian reputation. One member of Capital Baptist Church told the following story in front of the whole congregation.

> I made a significant mistake at work. I became sexually involved with a female co-worker. I knew it wasn't right. While the tryst did not progress into a relationship, my co-worker became pregnant from our encounter. I had to figure out what I should do next. Everyone at work found out about it. Some kidded me about my faith. After witnessing to my co-workers about Jesus, I had fathered a child out of the bonds of marriage. Needless to say, I felt embarrassed about the circumstances and took some deserved grief from my co-workers.

Then I got back on the right track. I knew what I had to
do. I took full responsibility and accepted my role as father
to the child. My daughter (from this relationship) is one
of the best gifts I have ever received. I treasure her and
support her. Although the situation could not be described
as God's best for me or for my Christian witness, I didn't
compound the damage. I did everything possible to make
the situation right and move on with my life. Eventually,
I left that employer and found another job.

This member's story touched many in the congregation. Everyone has seen his love for his daughter as he brings her to Sunday
School. His commitment to helping her grow up with a father in
her life is truly a positive outcome. Although the circumstances
temporarily blew up his witness at that company, over time he
proved how he intends to live his life: as a follower of Jesus.

Helping Others Get Back On the Right Track

When someone is in the process of making a significant mistake,
the Bible instructs us to attempt, with humility, to turn that
person back to the right path. "Brethren, if anyone among you
wanders from the truth, and someone turns him back, let him
know that he who turns a sinner from the error of his way will
save a soul from death and cover a multitude of sins" (James
5:19–20).

At work, this principle still applies. If we help a friend who
is falling into a bad attitude, our support may be the thing that
leads him or her back into many more years of successful service
with the employer. Gently encouraging a team member who is
feeling down after a major blunder could save that person a great
deal of self-doubt. Many times, the consequences of our errors
at work entirely rests with our supervisor. He or she can either
overlook it, dole out severe penalties, or do something in between.

When we are the supervisor in charge, it's important (when
possible) for us to pray through these situations before addressing

them. Our leadership should always be redemptive but may require the person who messed up to face some consequences. There are times when the only way to get through to someone about the seriousness of the error is to require him or her to face disciplinary action. I used formal discipline only a couple of times during my twenty years in management. Both times, the employee and the organization sorely needed action to be taken to rectify the unproductive behavior. And both times, it significantly improved the employee's conduct and performance as well as the organization's ability to function effectively.

Forgiving Others

There are times when our mistake will not be handled well by our supervisor or colleagues. We may have done everything possible to be honest and up front about our mistake. We may have worked to fix the problem we caused. Yet others might still hold the episode against us. Rivals might put us down or continually tease us about the blunder. In these cases, our only response is forgiveness.

> Repay no one evil for evil. Have regard for good things in the sight of all men. If it is possible, as much as depends on you, live peaceably with all men. Beloved, do not avenge yourselves, but rather give place to wrath; for it is written, 'Vengeance is Mine, I will repay,' says the Lord. Therefore 'if your enemy is hungry, feed him; if he is thirsty, give him a drink; for in so doing you will heap coals of fire on his head (Romans 12:17–20).

Trusting the Lord to have our back, even when we err, is the sign of a mature relationship with God.

Coming Back From Failure

Life deals us many blows. Sometimes we feel like fighters who have been beaten, vanquished, and permanently injured. Our career may be in shambles. Perhaps mistakes have compounded failures, which have piled on personal pain. We may feel like we have nothing left to give.

As always, the best place to turn is to the Lord. No matter what we've done or how others have reacted, God still loves us and has a plan to restore us. God always has another strategy for redemption, even if we've messed up the last one. The Lord is knowledge incarnate. Even if our situation seems hopeless, Jesus knows the answer. His Father invented work and knows what we can still do to make the world a better place and get paid for our labor.

God Can Miraculously Provide

When Jesus and Peter came to the town of Capernaum during their travels, the local tax man approached Peter and asked if Jesus would pay his temple tax. This particular "tax" was actually a scheme the local religious leaders used to rip off strangers who visited their area. Peter knew the disciples had no money at that moment and brought the issue to Jesus.

The Savior's response proved He always has one more miracle up his sleeve. He said to Peter, "Go to the sea, cast in a hook, and take the fish that comes up first. And when you have opened its mouth, you will find a piece of money; take that and give it to them for Me and you" (Matthew 17:27). If Jesus can cause a coin-laden fish to swim up to Peter on cue, He can come up with a new job for us or temporary provision apart from a job—if that is the true need.

No matter how down we've been, God's plan is to bring us back up. God is a future maker. He has hope for us. When we call out to Him, we will be amazed at the results.

> When the LORD brought back the captivity of Zion, we were like those who dream. Then our mouth was filled with laughter, and our tongue with singing. Then they said among the nations, 'The LORD has done great things for them.' The LORD has done great things for us, and we are glad. Bring back our captivity, O LORD, as the streams in the South. Those who sow in tears shall reap in joy. He who continually goes forth weeping, bearing seed

for sowing, shall doubtless come again with rejoicing, bringing his sheaves with him (Psalm 126:1–6).

A Major Miscalculation About Time

Perhaps the biggest mistake we can ever make is to put off a decision to serve Christ. Eventually, all of us will run out of time. The tricky part is that actuarial tables aren't reliable down to the individual level. Few of us know if we have another year to live or thirty more years. It is never a good idea to put off living for Jesus. Now is the right time to use our talents and energy to take care of His world. David wrote, "So teach us to number our days, that we may gain a heart of wisdom" (Psalm 90:12).

Summary

There is a difference between mistakes and sin. Sin is a subset of mistakes that involve disobedience to God's law. Work mistakes are often not sin, but they may require us to own up to the miscues to avoid harming our co-workers, supervisors, or the company as a whole. We should be encouraged that recovery is possible, even from mistakes that cost us our jobs. Moral failure is more serious, but it can be overcome through repentance and cleansing from God. In these instances, we must keep trusting God, keep loving God, and keep imitating God. Repentance may include restitution if our actions have materially hurt others. Our hope is that any persons we've wronged will forgive us, and as Christians, we owe forgiveness to those who have sinned against us. The most serious error anyone can ever make is to put off knowing Christ. At some point, all of us will run out of time on earth. It is imperative that we accept Jesus before we miss our opportunity.

Spotlight Feature

Johnny Curtis

As co-owners of Freedom Tree Service, Johnny Curtis and his brother operate their company in the DC suburbs according to Christian principles. The name of the company took shape in part from John 8:36: "Therefore if the Son makes you free, you shall be free indeed." The name also stems from their mother's commitment to be a freedom fighter for God and country.

From its inception, Johnny has run the firm according to biblical principles. "It sets us apart from some of the competition," he says. Perhaps pun intended, he notes that "trees are a shady business," and it is easy to shine if you treat people right. Johnny's Christian values have proven effective in his twelve years in business. "If you don't overcharge and you clean up after yourselves, the word spreads," he says.

"We have very good reviews on Angie's List and Yelp! because we treat people right."

Johnny doesn't insist that new hires to the company be acknowledged Christians, but he does explain to them that the business will be run by biblical principles. "It's good for business," he states. "Employees also see that we pray at the beginning of each work day. We huddle up to pass out the various job assignments for the day. At the conclusion of that meeting, I always lead a prayer and ask the Lord's blessing on the day."

Johnny has every intention of doing things God's way, yet mistakes still happen in both Christian and secular business. Freedom Tree has fourteen employees during the busiest season of the year, and multiple crews are in several locations. In one memorable incident, Johnny's nephew and another man were running a stump grinder to eliminate the remnants of a fallen tree. Johnny got a call from his nephew that day. "I think we dented a car," he said. Although the facts seemed sketchy, his nephew felt confident the stump grinder threw out a rock or other debris, which then hit a neighbor's vehicle.

After inspecting the car, it became obvious it had incurred other bumps and bruises besides just what would have been caused by the impact of the rock from the grinder. At first, Johnny asked his nephew if he was certain they had been responsible for the dent. When his nephew confirmed he thought they had done it, Johnny felt he had no choice but to offer to pay for the damage.

"In those moments, your integrity is challenged," Johnny says. "Would it be easier to pretend it didn't happen? Did anyone else see the incident? But I realized it isn't just about me. How would my nephew feel if I didn't handle it ethically? My witness was on the line." The result of notifying the neighbor cost the business $700.

"Biblical principles are the way to long-term success," Johnny says. Momentary temptations to take shortcuts may seem right in the short run, but people will see through us. The Bible is the way to lasting success. Scripture is the best business guidebook.

Spotlight Questions

What could you identify with in Johnny's story?

What action steps occurred to you about taking God to work?

Study Questions

1   Read James 5:16. What is a mistake you've made at work?

2   How did you handle the mistake? Did you admit it? Did you find forgiveness?

3   Read Galatians 1:10. What does it mean to be a people pleaser?

4   Why is it important to care more about pleasing God than pleasing other people?

5   How do you try to avoid being a people pleaser?

6   Read Romans 12:17–20. What is an on-the-job incident where you thought about repaying evil for evil?

7   What part does forgiveness play in living peaceably with others?

8   How does this passage recommend you treat those who have sinned against you?

9   Read Psalm 90:12. What does it mean to "number our days?"

10   How does remembering the limited time everyone will live lead you to pray about seemingly insignificant things?

11   Read James 5:19–20. Why should you help co-workers who are falling into bad attitudes or bad behaviors at work?

12   When was a time you helped someone at work who later gave you credit for turning him or her around from the wrong path that person was on?

Prayer

Lord, You understand my frailty better than I do. Please forgive me for mistakes I've made as a result of my sinful nature, desires, or actions. Grant me complete repentance of heart and mind that I might serve You in holiness. Because of Your grace to me, I forgive those who have sinned against me, and I pray You would not hold them accountable for those mistakes that harmed me. Show me how to make amends for those wrongs that I have committed against others. Grant me the integrity not to hide my sin but to bring it to You and allow You to completely heal me. For all these things, I thank You and live in Your debt. In the name of Jesus, Amen.

What will you do to take God to work this week?

Winning the Spiritual Endgame

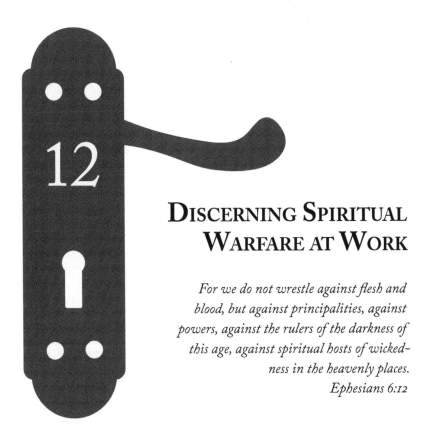

12

DISCERNING SPIRITUAL WARFARE AT WORK

For we do not wrestle against flesh and blood, but against principalities, against powers, against the rulers of the darkness of this age, against spiritual hosts of wickedness in the heavenly places.

Ephesians 6:12

QUIET FILLED THE OFFICE THAT DAY. After a morning chocked full of business calls, meetings, and paperwork, the files on my desk pointed to a long, boring afternoon of searching property records. While this task was not my favorite part of the contracting officer job, I knew it had to be done. Property management paperwork usually took a back seat to more time-sensitive matters, and on long-running contracts like the one before me, the property may have been transferred many times, creating a morass of intertwined claims and issues. Someone—me, in this case—eventually had to figure it all out so the contract file could be closed and the final payment made. While not complicated, the process proved tedious and time-consuming even with my trusty bottle of Diet Pepsi for company.

Several inches deep into the large brown file, eye-strain and tedium had induced an almost hypnotic state on my mind. Suddenly, I heard shouting coming from the nearby copier room. The male voice spoke in even tones, but the woman shrieked and screamed. Her voice became louder as she rebuked the devil and called out to God.

"Get behind me, Satan!" Brenda shouted. "You have no authority here. Take your evil host and get out of this office forever!"

"Yes, I'm the all-powerful one, your boss," Jason responded. "I'm ordering you to get back to your desk before I write you up for insubordination."

I peeked out of my office and saw Brenda running back to her desk along one wall of the large open area. She cried loudly, and tears ran down her face as she plopped dejectedly into her chair.

Jason stomped authoritatively across the large open area to his office. Once there, he slammed the metal and glass door, which echoed with a clunky reverberating sound. Although not usually in charge, he served as acting manager that afternoon while our mutual boss went across town for a meeting.

I returned to my desk and tried to get back into the large property file. A few minutes later, Janis, a co-worker, ducked into my office and closed the door behind her. In our small ten-person office, it took little effort to see who went where. I knew why Janis had come to see me and, most likely, so did everyone else on the staff.

Janis raised her eyebrows and gave me her best surprised look.

"What's going on out there?" I asked.

"Apparently, Brenda thinks Jason is the Antichrist of the Bible and is populating the office with his evil host of demons."

"That's interesting," I responded, not sure how to interpret any of this. Gossip wasn't my thing, and none of this sounded like something I wanted to jump into.

"Jason egged her on at first, because he found the whole thing ludicrous. He's not the most spiritual guy in the world, but I don't think he's in a position to become a world leader. So, I doubt he is the embodiment of Satan on earth. But I'm worried Brenda might get a gun and go postal."

My curiosity peaked at the idea that any of us might be in danger. "I hear you," I said. "I have my trusty government-issued tape dispenser if violence breaks out. My back-up security plan is to wail it at the shooter." My attempted humor did little to set Janis at ease. "Seriously though, the shouting is disruptive. Do you think Brenda will get into major trouble for the outburst? Jason *is* the manager in charge."

"Brenda claims she is going to file some kind of complaint because Jason harassed her. According to her, he comes into the copier room every time she goes in there to pray. That's how she discerned 'evil' was at work in the office. He claims he just needs to make copies and the timing has been a coincidence."

Our regular boss had left Jason in charge, but I wondered if he had the clout to actually take disciplinary action. Brenda's yelling at him certainly had to be considered inappropriate, if not insubordinate.

Later, I ended up in the copier room with Brenda. She brought up the situation to me and quickly became emotional. "You have to believe me," she said adamantly. "Jason and his evil host are at work in this office. He can't fool me. I know what's going on here. The devil is behind it."

I didn't know what to say. And I still don't.

The situation with Brenda and Jason may sound extreme, but it reflects actual events that happened during my career with the federal government. What began as an attempt at humor by Jason turned into a volatile situation with Brenda. She literally believed that Jason, a rather mild-mannered-looking engineer, represented a serious evil presence, if not the Antichrist described in the book of Revelation.

Although at the time I had been a Christian for fifteen years, I felt none of the evil my co-worker sensed. Jason seemed like a normal guy, though with a goofy sense of humor. He claimed to be a practicing Catholic. As I prayed about the situation, my gut told me personality conflict gone awry, more so than legitimate spiritual warfare.

Although neither employee suffered serious consequences for the outburst, Brenda soon accepted another job elsewhere, which included a pay bump. I lost touch with her when she transferred out. Only God knows for sure, but time has proven that Jason is not the Antichrist of the Bible. His career continued to flourish as he accepted a promotion in another city and faded into government oblivion.

Personality Conflict or Spiritual Warfare?

As followers of Christ, we are called to be aware of spiritual forces. As mentioned previously, Paul put it this way: "For we do not wrestle against flesh and blood, but against principalities, against powers, against the rulers of the darkness of this age, against spiritual hosts of wickedness in the heavenly places" (Ephesians 6:12). So, how do we tell the difference between a personality conflict, like the one described above, and real spiritual conflict?

We pray and ask God for discernment. He must grant us spiritual eyes to see beyond the personalities to understand if there is more at work in the spiritual realm. The Holy Spirit inside us has many purposes, and one of these may be to help us figure out what's going on spiritually and how we should pray. The name of Jesus is greater than any force in the universe. As believers, we have authority, granted by Jesus, to clear away any evil spiritual forces in our workplaces. Jesus said, "Behold, I give you the authority to trample on serpents and scorpions, and over all the power of the enemy, and nothing shall by any means hurt you" (Luke 10:19).

Think that over. God intended for us to bring the light of Jesus into our workplace, shine it all over, and cause dark forces to flee. Although this authority is significant, it barely registers in comparison to our eternal salvation. That is the most amazing gift. Jesus drove this point home when He said,

> I saw Satan fall like lightning from heaven. Behold, I give you the authority to trample on serpents and scorpions, and over all the power of the enemy, and nothing shall by any means hurt you. Nevertheless, do not rejoice in this, that the spirits are subject to you, but rather rejoice because your names are written in heaven (Luke 10:18–20).

If our motives are pure and we continually get resistance to the good things we are trying to accomplish, we need to bring the matter to the LORD. He will teach us to pray for peace, order, and success at our workplace. God knows everything that is going on. We don't know and probably *won't* know exactly how much of our conflict is rooted in spiritual opposition. But God may grant us a small part to play in bringing spiritual peace to our own corner of the company, government organization, or other place of employment.

We have to realize that not everyone who rubs us the wrong way is necessarily overcome with evil. It is a big, beautiful world with all kinds of personalities in it. People come to work from an infinite number of environmental factors that have shaped their personalities. An angry father, a distant mother, a mentally ill brother, or a drug-addicted aunt may have taught your co-worker coping mechanisms that are not helpful. This doesn't make them evil. But when their human frailty rubs up against our own immaturity, fireworks can ignite. The key is to bring these situations to God in prayer.

Pray For Spiritual Wisdom

God does not want His children to be ignorant of the spiritual forces in the world around us. He also doesn't want us to fear them. Jesus is LORD of all because He conquered death and the grave. There is no evil that can overcome Christ. The king of evil tried to subdue God's Son but failed. Our charge is to rest in the wisdom of Scripture and rely on the guidance of God's Spirit to discern what's going on around us. Paul prayed that "the God of our LORD Jesus Christ, the Father of glory, may give to you the spirit of wisdom and revelation in the knowledge of Him" (Ephesians 1:17).

Careful With Saying, "God Told Me"

When it comes to God and the world of work, Christians must be careful of two extremes. At the one extreme is a totally secular workplace where believers check their faith at the door, put their heads down, and work without thoughts of God until the closing bell rings. At the other extreme is an overly spiritualized view where believers perceive that every action is prompted by either God or the devil.

While God wants us to pray without ceasing, He doesn't expect us to find spiritual nuggets in every shovel of dirt we scoop. There lurks neither a demon behind every setback nor an angel guiding our every success. Applying God's principles to our work will likely lead us to many successes and help us overcome challenges as well. The LORD will use our difficulties to build our character and refine our personalities to be more like Jesus.

As we try to live being more aware of God at our workplaces, we may be tempted to believe that God is giving us all kinds of advice for other people. This can happen, but more often we just end up giving out our own advice to our co-workers and attribute it to God. The practice of saying, "God told me," can be spiritually hazardous for ourselves and for the recipient of the advice.

If God really did say something to us for the other person, that's fine. But if God's voice wasn't truly behind the word of advice, the recipient may become confused or even undertake some activity that is definitely not in God's plan for them. More often, God speaks individually and directly to His children through Scripture, sermons, or other teachings. He does use conversations with other believers, but usually this is to confirm the point His Holy Spirit has already shown to that person. For this reason, if we have an *opinion* we want to share with a friend, we need to do so without attributing it to God.

As brothers and sisters in the LORD, God may lead us to carefully give counsel with another believer, particularly in an area where we have experience. We need to do so humbly and without getting hung up about whether the advice is immediately well received. Sometimes, people need to think about a matter and mull it over in light of Scripture.

Obviously, the Bible is a sure foundation and authoritative voice—more so than what people say. But whatever the source, God will confirm His words to us in our hearts. "My sheep hear My voice, and I know them, and they follow Me" (John 10:27). God is good, and He wants us to clearly understand the right path He wants us to take.

Indicators Of Spiritual Warfare

Previously, we asserted that most work problems are people problems. This is certainly true on a human level. By working through our issues with other people, we grow, learn about ourselves, and come to understand more about God. But beyond the human world we see is a world of spiritual forces. The key verse for this chapter reminds us that our battle as Christians is really not against other people but against principalities, powers, rulers of the darkness of this age, and spiritual hosts of wickedness in the heavenly places.

This realization matters, because our tendency is to look at our roadblocks as only skin deep. Once we've embraced our God-given giftedness and begin taking care of His world, we become partners with Him in all that is good and right. As we serve other people in the name of Jesus, our witness cries out "there is a God" and "He loves you."

Why on earth would anyone not support someone doing good and bringing glory to God? The answer is simple: there are enemies of God. Evil exists, and it wants to supplant and oppose those who long for God's glory, His praise, and His power to be released. Satan and his spirits work through people to discredit God and His people. He does not want God's kingdom to pre- vail in heaven or on earth. But how can we know whether our opposition is truly supernatural? We can't know for sure, but here are some warning signs:

- Our efforts meet constant resistance for no logical reason.
- Those who oppose us make it personal and attack us instead of the proposed solution or change.
- No matter how much we attempt to bring clarity, the proj- ect or service is repeatedly thrown into confusion.
- The opposition uses discouragement and often makes us want to quit.

At this point, you may be considering setting the book down and going for a walk. Hang in there with us. This book about taking God into the workplace would not be complete without an understanding of those times when normal human measures don't fix our problems. As the world continues to become more corrupt and more decadent, Christians need to know, more than ever, how to respond to assaults on their belief system.

Spiritual Battle

Before His death, Jesus prayed for those of us who would believe on His name in the future. Just as Jesus did nothing without the Father's approval, we will find power and beauty as we increase our unity with God and with other believers.

In a poignant and beautiful prayer, Jesus showed His com- passion for us as we shine His light into a dark and sometimes cruel world. His compassion and understanding of us offers great encouragement. His prayer went like this:

> I do not pray for these alone, but also for those who will believe in Me through their word; that they all may be one, as You, Father, are in Me, and I in You; that they also may be one in Us, that the world may believe that You sent Me. And the glory which You gave Me, I have given them, that they may be one just as We are one: I in them, and You in Me; that they may be made perfect in one, and that the world may know that You have sent Me, and have loved them as You have loved Me (John 17:20–23).

God knew we would face spiritual battles, so He also offers us spiritual armor to help us at work and beyond. "Put on the whole armor of God, that you may be able to stand against the wiles of the devil... Therefore take up the whole armor of God, that you may be able to withstand in the evil day, and having done all, to stand" (Ephesians 6:11, 13).

Praying through our business situations will give God an opportunity to show us how to deal with the spiritual forces we encounter. Our unity with God and His purpose will overcome many obstacles. Again and again in my career with the government, I learned the importance of praying before meetings. When I remembered to do so, it often amazed me how much more God accomplished during the meeting.

If you are experiencing opposition and it appears to be spiritual, don't be afraid to take authority over any power or principality in the name of Jesus. Order it to go and never return by the power of Jesus.

Sometimes we know all the right things to do. We've prayed and trusted God for the result. We've taken authority over evil and exercised our faith. In these situations, the only thing left to do is stand and trust that God is working to fix our problem.

> Stand therefore, having girded your waist with truth, having put on the breastplate of righteousness, and having shod your feet with the preparation of the gospel of peace; above all, taking

the shield of faith with which you will be able to quench all the fiery darts of the wicked one. And take the helmet of salvation, and the sword of the Spirit, which is the word of God (Ephesians 6:14–17).

Like a sports team that slacked off on practice, sometimes it takes losing to remind us of the power of prayer and Bible study. When the fiery darts start flying at work, they often drive us back to our knees to talk it over with the LORD.

Be careful about taking personal advice from unbelievers at work. Those who don't share our worldview may suggest paths that would lead us away from God. Many marriages have been derailed when one partner or another listened to ungodly advice at work.

Indicators and Remedies For Personality Conflicts

There are probably an infinite number of reasons why two people might immediately like or dislike each other. Reasons for disliking another person are infinite: looks like someone who hurt us once, smells like our ex-boyfriend or uses sarcasm inappropriately. Whatever the cause, as Christians we have a calling to try to live peacefully with our colleagues and respect the authority of our bosses.

In those situations where we find ourselves just wanting to get away from another person, it is usually worth the time to figure why we are reacting this way. God will help us figure it out if we invite Him into the situation. He will even help us to love the "unlovable" people if we garner the courage to ask for His help.

One practical remedy for resolving a personality conflict includes developing empathy for the other person. Try to figure out what might have bent that person in the direction that annoys you, and then use that knowledge to give that person grace should he or she trespass on one of your boundaries. If you don't know the person well, take a few minutes to chat with him or her. Sometimes a few minutes waiting for a meeting to start can provide you with valuable insights. If you learn things about the person that are admirable, it may counteract some of your aversion to him or her. Finally, try to imagine what Jesus might see in the person. He tended to find the good or the potential in almost everyone.

Whether you are encountering legitimate spiritual warfare or just a personality conflict, use your spiritual armor and your relationship with God to find out the best way to handle it.

Have No Fellowship

To adopt the Christian walk is to cast off our sinful past. When we separate our Christian walk and our life at work, we run the risk of living out our work hours apart from the benefits and protection of our faith. Whether we like to admit it or not, we need our faith at work—maybe more so than when we are safely in our homes on the couch.

Work environments sometimes include pockets of spiritual wickedness. Those under the power of the evil one may try to draw us into conversations, thoughts, and actions that are anathema to our commitment to Christ. Living out the light that is within us has the potential to drive out the darkness, but it isn't automatic. Our charge is to recognize when we have stepped near the boundaries of darkness and refuse to proceed into fellowship with evil.

> For you were once darkness, but now you are light in the LORD. Walk as children of light (for the fruit of the Spirit is in all goodness, righteousness, and truth), finding out what is acceptable to the LORD. And have no fellowship with the unfruitful works of darkness, but rather expose them. For it is shameful even to speak of those things which are done by them in secret. But all things that are exposed are made manifest by the light, for whatever makes manifest is light (Ephesians 5:8–13).

This doesn't mean you can't speak to, or work with, non-Christian people. It just means that some situations, some conversations, and some joking around aren't right for you. Listen to the Holy Spirit within you to discern when it's time to withdraw your fellowship from people who are tearing you down or harming your faith. God will talk to you. Just yield to His quiet suggestions and head back to your desk or work area.

The same advice applies when dealing with Christians who have fallen for false teaching or false teachers. If you find yourself in serious disagreement with another professing Christian about a point of doctrine, there may be a time when you should agree to disagree and move on. Arguing seldom changes the mind of another person, unless God does the work.

Make sure you understand the difference between false teaching and different points of emphasis. Paul used the analogy of a body in 1 Corinthians 12:12–31 to describe the church, and it has many parts. He warns believers not to think that every person will have the same function in the body of Christ. Hands don't do what feet are supposed to do.

Every person in the body came from a spiritual background or heritage. If you view that heritage as particularly rich or safe, you may be quick to judge others who don't understand every doctrine the same way you see it. The Bible gives you a firm foundation for your beliefs. If you find allies in the Christian faith at work, don't waste the resource of their fellowship over one or two less important doctrines that may separate you.

Beating Discouragement With Joy

One of the enemy's most common weapons is discouragement. Every time you love someone in the name of the Father, you are bringing His kingdom to the earth. By witnessing to others with your love and care for them, you are acting as a mighty force for good. The secret of a successful Christian life is to keep going, keep doing good, keep loving, and keep showing people the Jesus inside of you. "But as for you, brethren, do not grow weary in doing good" (2 Thessalonians 3:13).

Work and Our Spiritual Life

God wants us to work, take care of His world, and enjoy the fruit of our labor. The Christian worker is intended to be a witness of God's love, grace, and provision. Don't underestimate the good you are doing by living an authentic Christian life at your job. Chances are you are doing a world of good in the physical and spiritual realms.

> But we urge you, brethren, that you increase more and more; that you also aspire to lead a quiet life, to mind your own business, and to work with your own hands, as we commanded you, that you may walk properly toward those who are outside, and that you may lack nothing (1 Thessalonians 4:10–12).

Restoring Order

Spiritual battles and personality conflicts strain relationships and upset the orderliness of our workplace. Words are said that can't be taken back, and relationships can be badly damaged. As salt and light, Christians should be willing to speak up when things aren't going well. At the Department of Homeland Security, I got a reputation as a turn-around specialist for our troubled business units. This began with reshaping a single underperforming division. Later, my bosses asked me to take over other struggling divisions and improve their performance and morale. With God's help, I used this six-part approach to achieve these goals.

1. Calm Everyone Down

First, I calmed everyone down and worked to promote an atmosphere of peace in the office. At that point I had more than ten years of management experience under my belt, and God used that preparation for the challenges I faced. In my first post as a manager at the Department of Homeland Security, I quickly detected a lot of tension and even yelling back and forth in the office. Employees gossiped about each other, the customers, and management. By refocusing everyone on the tasks at hand and shutting down the gossip, internal relations and relationships with our customers greatly improved. I reminded my folks that professional conduct must be demonstrated at all times. The new requirement to keep their voices at a normal volume eventually took hold. After a couple of months, the office atmosphere became noticeably more peaceful and quiet.

2. Emphasize the Importance Of the Mission and Customer Service

The Department of Homeland Security workforce was united by a common goal of protecting their families, friends, and fellow countrymen. The department was formed after the September 11, 2001 terrorist attacks. Its mission was to protect the United States homeland from natural and manmade threats. In the office, I asked the employees to work more closely with their customers to eliminate some of the "us versus them" mentalities. As the customers grew to understand our needs in trying to serve them, we all became better at producing the end product: quality contracts for goods and services. The mission gave everyone a vision of where the future might lead and took away some of the fear that our efforts would be ineffective.

3. Value Quality Work

When people feel appreciated, they go to great lengths to reward their managers and their organization with a great volume and quality of work. Admittedly, at one point I encouraged a couple of key trouble makers to job hunt. These individuals had become rigid in their opinions and were the first to gossip when things didn't go their way. Even worse, they encouraged others to take sides in a non-existent war of popularity. Fortunately, they found comparable employment where, hopefully, they were more content. Beyond these bad apples, I valued and rewarded the contributions of everyone else. Understaffing posed the biggest problem when I first took over as a division director, and several of the employees continued doing heroic things to keep up with the demands of our customers.

4. Stick Up For Important Principles

Employees want to follow leaders who stick to admirable principles. When a new president appointed new leadership at the Department of Homeland Security, political types at the top of the organization promulgated a controversial terror watch list. It included many conservative organizations, including my MBA alma mater, Regent University, founded by Pat Robertson. I suspected the school had made the list because of Robertson's conservative beliefs.

Any organization that embraced biblical standards was perceived as a threat by the new leadership. I and dozens of other workers at the Department of Homeland Security used our positions to push back on this outrageous persecution of Christian organizations. While not all of my employees agreed with my political bent, they understood the importance of leaving politics out of things like defining terrorist organizations.

5. Make It Clear That People Matter

Due to inadequate staffing at the Department of Homeland Security and the demands of our mission, some of the employees began breaking down physically and mentally. One of my first acts as the new boss involved supporting vacations and sick leave. Although we needed more hands and the vacation time seemed counterproductive, I knew that fresh employees would accomplish a lot more than worn-out troops. It was hard for the people to be at their best when they were exhausted and getting them out of the office for needed breaks changed a lot of attitudes.

6. Share Your Faith Judiciously

God led me to share my faith in specific ways with specific individuals, though only rarely and in key moments of their lives. Being the boss meant people told me things about their personal situations and problems. On occasion, this opened doors for me to offer hope, encouragement, or other guidance. If the employee or colleague came from a Christian background,

I would offer to pray for him or her. In all cases, I tried to point the person to the LORD.

Only a few times over the years did this end badly. One time, a gay employee facing a difficult personal situation took offense at the mention of God. He had been raised by a father who served as a pastor. My employee had grown up playing piano in church. When I tried to bring up God, he screamed and warned me to never to broach the subject again. I respected his request, but I still prayed for him often.

In my thirty-three-year career with the federal government, I experienced many ups and downs. During my twenty-plus years in management, I faced serious situations that caused great stress and even physical difficulty. However, the blessings far outweighed the problems. The friendly faces greatly outnumbered the angry ones, and the joy of the LORD lifted me up day by day. While some took my demeanor to mean that I never had a serious problem, the truth is that I knew the problem solver. God always made Himself available to help sort out any situation. Business meetings went much better when I prayed first. God became a partner in many business dealings and brought numerous promotions, awards, and adventures.

Summary

The Christian's fight is usually not against a flesh and blood enemy, so we must depend on God's help to fight our spiritual battles. Half the battle is simply being aware that spiritual forces may oppose us as we attempt to care for the world in Jesus' name. We may need to pray for discernment so we can tell the difference between a simple personality conflict and spiritual opposition. Some addictions, certain sins, and various agendas can't be overcome simply by using our human efforts. We must call on the LORD in prayer for spiritual wisdom.

Getting prepared means putting on the whole armor of God as described in Ephesians 6:10–20. The major offensive weapons are God's Word and the Holy Spirit. The good news is that Jesus already came and won the war. He conquered the grave, and when we are willing to submit our lives to Him, our enemies have little power except to temporarily disrupt God's plan as it unfolds through Christ's followers.

Spotlight Feature
Deby Allen

Deby Allen, the owner/operator of Special Effects Styling Salon in New Carlisle, Ohio, takes her faith to work each day. Although she has run the salon for twenty-seven years, her spiritual awakening came eighteen years ago. She credits one of her longtime employees for praying Christ into their workplace. "I'm sure she wore out the knees of her pants praying for me," Deby says. Since that time, she has tried to put God first in everything.

Deby grew tired of the negativity of the outside world and the gossip that dominated her profession. So, she decided to change the music to a Christian station, KLOVE radio. The positive Christian music and her own decision to put God in charge changed the atmosphere of her salon and led to big results. "I got so tired of all the negative stuff," Deby says. "God just changed everything. Switching to KLOVE, it got really peaceful in the shop. I don't have to worry about trashy commercials. People like the uplifting messages. It's like getting away from the outside world and all the bad things that are happening."

In addition to changing the radio station, Deby tries to make Special Effects a peaceful oasis. "We stopped nitpicking, gossiping, and using inappropriate language. Bringing God into the picture transformed Special Effects." Subscribing to fifteen magazine subscriptions, Deby throws out any with trashy covers.

God taught Deby to get her priorities in order. "He told me to put Him first," she says. "People second. I'm third. I pray for my clients and for my staff. The day goes much better when I do it that way. Everything flows better. I ask God to guard and guide my words, thoughts, and deeds."

When things go wrong for a client, Deby puts her faith in action by trying her best to fix any missteps. "With long-time clients, there aren't many problems," she says. "But occasionally, a newer client will not like something, and we find a way to fix it." This might mean not charging for a particular treatment or re-dying someone's hair a different color. The key is to treat others fairly, as we would want to be treated, she says.

Eighteen years ago, Deby learned that putting God first meant making major changes in the way she ran her business. "It changes how you deal with money," she says. "It keeps you honest. I don't want to cheat God. Nobody knows about the little things, but God does. Follow His Word in all your practices. I've learned from trusting Him that I don't need to comment when people bring up a gossipy subject. I don't need to share it or get into that conversation."

To Deby's surprise, over the years God has done amazing things in the lives of her staff and her clients. Working in a Christian environment even led one of her employees to faith in Jesus. The breakthrough came through a gradual process. "She started going to church," she says, "and made a profession of faith, eventually being baptized." Nothing beats the feeling of helping someone find the LORD through your business.

Spotlight Questions

What could you identify with in Deby's story?

What action steps occurred to you about taking God to work?

Study Questions

1   *Read Ephesians 6:12.* What comes to mind when you imagine a spiritual battle?

2   Why do you think the Bible states that you are not wrestling against flesh and blood but against principalities, powers, and rulers of the darkness of this age?

3   How can prayer help you battle against unseen powers?

4   *Read 2 Corinthians 10:4.* Why do you think Paul said the Christian's weapons are not carnal?

5   What spiritual weapons does the Christian possess that could help tear down strongholds?

6   What does it mean to bring thoughts into the captivity of Christ?

7   *Read 1 Timothy 1:18–19.* In what ways do Christians today wage warfare in the workplace?

8   Faith and a good conscience will help to wage warfare. How has this worked for you?

9   *Read 1 Thessalonians 4:10–12.* How does living peaceably with all men fit in with waging spiritual warfare?

10 How can waging spiritual warfare actually contribute to your reputation with those outside the Christian faith?

11 *Read 2 Timothy 2:4.* What worldly entanglements could prevent you from being a good soldier for Christ?

12 How can you be a good spiritual soldier in your workplace this week?

Prayer

Dear God, thank You for each of the co-workers, bosses, and employees that You have placed in my world. Thank You for those easy-to-get-along-with colleagues and also for those who rubbed me the wrong way. Thank You for the lessons I learned from the pleasant people I came to call friends and for the difficult individuals who may have tried purposefully to harm me. Your wisdom is higher than mine. My cognitive powers are tiny compared with the Creator of the Universe. Even so, I humbly ask that You grant me the discernment to know the root causes of any personality conflicts, disagreements, and spiritual battles that come my way. Remind me through Your Holy Spirit to bring each situation to You, listen at Your feet, and glean answers from Your Holy Scriptures. Allow me to live at peace with all men and women, as far as possible, while holding true to my Christian values. In the name of Jesus, amen.

What will you do to take God to work this week?

SHOULD CHRISTIANS RETIRE?

Surely there is a reward for the righteous;
surely He is God who judges in the earth.
Psalm 58:11

MILESTONES CAN BE BEAUTIFUL. When I look back over a thirty-three-year career, I can point to hundreds of times when I believe God blessed me because of my relationship with Him. From the time in my twenties when I yielded my work life to God, until my eventual retirement with Homeland Security at the end of 2015, I can see God's hand directing me at each twist and turn. Even when I made or contemplated huge mistakes, He spoke to me in one way or another and often redirected my path.

In my years with the government, I saw major reorganizations, received a wall full of awards, got promoted numerous times, traveled to nearly every major city in the continental

U.S., hugged employees with cancer, cried with co-workers at funerals, and experienced a lifetime of memories. All the laughter I experienced and generated through those thirty-three years could fill a laugh-track three days long.

Working for research and science organizations allowed me to preview amazing technological advances, work with very smart people, and understand the diversity of mankind a little better. (Did you know that most scientists don't like to chitchat on the elevator?) From a naval ship that could travel at sixty knots, to technology that could make planes invisible to radar, every day became a learning experience. One of my favorite projects involved merging two different types of body armor to improve protection of our warfighters.

But even with all these exciting programs, the best part remained the people. My ability as a manager to speak into the lives of employees and colleagues, using a biblical perspective, probably amounted to my most important contribution. Many of my Christian co-workers and employees did the same for me.

What Do You Hope to Accomplish With Your Life?

At the beginning of our careers, most of us merely want to earn a living. Perhaps we have no idea where we even want to live. Thirty or forty years sounds like an eternity to a twenty-year-old. We don't yet understand the value of work or why it's important, and we may look at the prospects of forty years behind a desk as depressing and even daunting.

However, over time and with maturity, we come to realize the beauty of God's plan regarding work. In addition to supporting ourselves and our families, we find our work to be an extension of God's care for people, places, and things. At some point, retirement will come into sight—maybe ten years or less into the future. It's time to think about our career end game.

When you reach the terminus of your career, what accomplishments will be significant to you? To God? To those you love?

What is the type of contribution that will make you feel you wisely spent your most important resource here on earth—*time*? Will you be proud of building a large company or founding a nonprofit organization? Will you feel good about policies you developed that made things better for the poor or elderly?

Perhaps you will be proud of a new scientific discovery that brought healing to millions of people or the fact you created new jobs for hundreds or thousands of people. You may even take satisfaction from helping an employer earn billions of dollars because of some innovation you developed. Regardless, we hope this book has helped you evaluate or re-evaluate how you would like to help care for God's world.

If you are still far from retirement, the good news is you can alter the trajectory of your career. Even though the first part may have been all about you, the rest of your career can be all about God and helping Him care for His Creation.

Perspective

When we are in the middle of the forest, it can be difficult to gain perspective about the expanse of our career. At work, our opinion may only matter because of our rank or position. Five minutes after we retire—sometimes sooner—loyal employees and even friends will likely turn their attention to our successors. Think about it. Do your current employees spend hours worrying about what previous bosses or departed co-workers think of changes to the organization? They obviously don't give it more than a passing thought. So, what is really important to you? Friendships? Character? Souls won to Christ? Employees mentored? Lives nurtured? The way you cared for God's world through your job?

Our partnership with the Almighty unlocks untold blessings on those we serve. In no way are we equal partners or even deserving of our supporting roles, but God chooses to give us a part to play. As we are filled with the love He birthed in us, it is our incredible opportunity to love the world through our work. When we say goodbye to our workplace or our career, perhaps the most important thing is to know we tried our best to please God each day. The everyday miracles created by a surrendered life reveal the best way to maximize our talents: one day at a time.

The Calling of Our Partnership

Our inadequacy to fulfill this calling on our own should drive us to our knees in prayer. "Therefore I exhort first of all that supplications, prayers, intercessions, and giving of thanks be made for all men" (1 Timothy 2:1). Not every day on earth will be an adventure in paradise. Our efforts will sometimes be misunderstood. Our concern will sometimes be mislabeled as micro-management. Our acts of love will sometimes be spurned. Still, we must carry on with our divine purpose of caring for others through our work. This calling transcends our thirty to forty years in a "job." It is a lifetime calling. In the process, we may need take up more than a cross or two along the way.

> And he who does not take his cross and follow after Me is not worthy of Me. He who finds his life will lose it, and he who loses his life for My sake will find it. He who receives you receives Me, and he who receives Me receives Him who sent Me. He who receives a prophet in the name of a prophet shall receive a prophet's reward. And he who receives a righteous man in the name of a righteous man shall receive a righteous man's reward. And whoever gives one of these little ones only a cup of cold water in the name of a disciple, assuredly, I say to you, he shall by no means lose his reward (Matthew 10:38–41).

This passage is meant to reassure us that when we feel deprived of some earthly reward, God will eventually make it worthwhile. There will be instances when our calling causes us to miss time with family, a personal convenience, or some leisure-time activity. No matter how balanced we try to live, serving others exacts a price. It is unrealistic to think fulfilling our calling will come without a cost, but God wants us to know that none of our efforts in His name will be wasted. We will reap a reward for the times we give our best to care for others. That's why it is essential to connect our earthly job to our heavenly calling of caring for creation.

Memories Make the Best Mementos

More than a few workers have been underwhelmed by the farewell presents given at their retirement. What gift could sum up a career full of experiences, memories, and toil? A gold watch used to be the typical retirement gift. But in truth, by the time we get to retirement, most tangible mementos hold little value. If anything, we are thinking of downsizing, not collecting a bunch of additional hardware to display or store.

The best remembrances of a career well spent are memories, triggered by photos. As you go along in your career, make sure to collect a few snapshots. Document the big occasions and the everyday fun. Some of my favorite work moments probably have been forgotten, but my most cherished possessions from work are almost always photos. A picture is just a quick moment of time, but takes me back to the people, places, and fun that punctuated the hard work and accomplishment. So, take note of milestones reached, projects successfully completed, and happy moments at the holiday party or company picnic. Later, you will be glad to have the reminders of precious people you've known and mountains you've climbed.

Transition Preparation

Many of us go through a great deal of preparation to begin our work life or progress to the journeyman level. For those in professional careers, this meant lots of education. After thirteen years of elementary and secondary school, we may have headed off to college for four or five more years. Then we might have chosen an internship to stick a toe in the water of our chosen career. Somewhere in our mid-career, we might have gone back to school for even more study in the form of a Master's Degree.

For those in the trades, our jobs might have required technical school training or on-the-job instruction. Perhaps we began in our field shortly after high school. Years of learning or apprenticeship may have led to us achieving great skill in our trade. By putting in long days and showing great hustle, we built a business either for ourselves or our employer.

Throughout our working years, we likely spent hours understanding the financial implications of retirement and investing for it. Now, we need to show that same kind of preparation and interest in the activities that will follow our eventual retirement. Just because our employer and society agree on an age range as to when we *may* retire, it doesn't mean we *should* retire from a particular job or field. Before selecting a date, we need to pray it out, leave the decision to God, and make sure we are ready for another adventure—another phase of life.

Leisure time can get old fast. Many retirees find that painting watercolors is not as fascinating as they hoped. Staying home and watching television will lose its allure quickly. Depending on the rigors of your job, you may well enjoy a few months at a slower pace before launching into your second act. The important thing is to explore and again find your place of ministry to God's world.

Retirement for the Christian should just be a transition to a different type of service. It may not involve the same rigid schedule or demands of a nine-to-five job, but God knows many ways you can useful. He wants to plug you into your next opportunity. If you follow Him, even in retirement, He just might make it the most eternally productive time of your life.

Concrete Steps to Finding Your New Passion

Check Out the United Way Website in Your Area
The United Way has an exhaustive list of volunteer activities.

I found my first volunteer organization, the Pediatric Aids Care Program (PACP), through the federal employee equivalent of United Way. I decided that if I gave my money to PACP, perhaps I could give my time there as well. If I hadn't looked at the federal website or checked out their booklet, I wouldn't have known PACP existed. Do some research and stick a toe in before jumping in with both feet.

Take a Class
Perhaps you will discover your true passion has nothing to do with your previous career. A painting class, writer's conference, or woodworking seminar may be just the thing to get you started.

Go Deeper With Your Church
If you are like most folks, work may have interfered with some of your desired church activities. For example, you may not have been able to serve in Vacation Bible School because you were too busy with your primary career. Rethink some of those "never" choices you made when you were working and decide what you can do with your additional availability.

Try a Short-term Missions Trip
Maybe God is leading you to help out a ministry in another part of the world. If so, consider a short-term missions trip where you could help build a structure, feed the hungry, or teach a course. You may not choose to dive into full-time missionary work, but perhaps you can become an advocate for the ministry in your hometown and beyond.

Take Care Of a Family Member
Perhaps one of your dreams for retirement is to be available to care for a family member. God's economy is not like our own, and not all service projects need to be national in scale. Perhaps watching your grandchildren after school is the best use of your time to help them get started well on life's journey.

Get a Part-time Job

Maybe you enjoyed your career and felt ready for retirement but not ready to stop working completely. After retirement, I drove for Uber and Lyft, though it paid much less than I received from my federal job. I used it for five months as research for my first novel—the riders and experiences provided much fodder for a mystery I wanted to write about a Christian Uber driver who wandered into a murder scene and got accused of the crime.

Try Out For a Play or a Movie

Have you always harbored secret desires to do something artistic? If so, use retirement to explore those passions. Perhaps you will find an aptitude that you didn't know existed in you.

Teach or Consult

You will have gained a wealth of experience after a career of working in a certain industry or trade. Put that experience to use by teaching at a community college or online. Or perhaps you could consult and earn extra money in retirement. Depending on your field, you may be paid handsomely to work on special projects for your old firm or another in the same industry.

Never Done Working

Until God calls you to your eternal home, you have not completed your earthly work. Retirement from a career is merely a gateway to your next assignment. As long as there are hurting people, churches with open doors, neighborhoods with untended public gardens, or town councils with vacancies, there will be plenty for you to do. As long as there are at-risk youth needing a tutor, books that need to be written, or disabled folks who need a meal and a smile, you need never want for work.

Finishing your life strong requires diligence. Retiring from a career should just be a transition to even more rewarding service. You are wiser now and know your gifts, talents, and abilities better than when you started. Many have started new ministries and nonprofit organizations in retirement. Others have launched new businesses with their first retirement checks. Whatever you do, pick something that will help you continue to take care of God's world. Jesus' cause is too important for you to rest on your laurels. "Look to yourselves, that we do not lose those things we worked for, but that we may receive a full reward" (2 John 1:8).

Perhaps you began this study feeling you are coasting on autopilot in your job. Your salary is a necessity, and you didn't see any reasonable alternatives to your chosen career. In this study, we have not suggested that anyone must or even should leave his or her current employment. The choice is between you, the Lord, and those who depend on you. But know that the Lord may have something better for you out there—and it is always okay to ask Him.

Throughout these chapters, our heart has been to help you see that by changing your perspective, your current workplace could become the ideal place for you and God to take care of people. If you are sure it's time to go, I hope you've gathered courage to look around, with God's help. Life is a vapor, so get on with whatever your divine purpose may require. As James wrote, "Whereas you do not know what will happen tomorrow. For what is your life? It is even a vapor that appears for a little time and then vanishes away" (James 4:14).

God knows everything you need, and He's even aware of the things you want. He won't keep any good thing from you, but He might recommend a different timetable than the one you have in mind. Trust me, His timing is a lot better than yours! There is no safer ride than a journey wrapped in the arms of the Father.

Heaven

The main feature in heaven is God's presence. "He will dwell with them, and they shall be His people, and God Himself will be with them and be their God. And God will wipe away every tear from their eyes; there shall be no more death, nor sorrow, nor crying; and there shall be no more pain, for the former things have passed away" (Revelation 21:3–4). Can you imagine a world without death or even sorrow?

Our sinful lives before we came to Christ led us nowhere, but the fruit of our resurrected life in Christ will lead us to holiness and eventually eternal life in heaven. Our work for the kingdom is an outgrowth of the eternal life that Jesus bought for us. The journey leads to heaven, with many interesting stops along the way. The Holy Spirit within us is a deposit, showing God's good faith to eventually bring us to Himself.

Our work lives become a symphony as we yield this important part of our existence to the Maestro of the Universe. "But now having been set free from sin, and having become slaves of God, you have your fruit to holiness, and the end, everlasting life. For the wages of sin is death, but the gift of God is eternal life in Christ Jesus our Lord" (Romans 6:21–23).

God's Approval

When it comes down to it, God's approval is the best recognition for our work. No person or group knows more about our accomplishments, our unrealized potential, or our motives than God. He sees the inside and the outside of us. He knows whether our accomplishments are made of eternal gold, silver, or something less valuable. Others may give us more credit than is due, or they might not recognize the importance of our intangible contributions. But when our work life comes before the ultimate Judge, He will know everything He needs to know. All we want to hear is, "Well done, good and faithful servant."

Summary

Before retirement sneaks up on us, it's important for us to review what we hope to accomplish during our work years. Perspective can help us realize what is really valuable and what is not. Our partnership with God, while an unequal one, gives us the possibility of adventure, joy, and fulfillment in our careers. Memories will be our best mementos, so we need to make sure to take snapshots so we can remember those with whom we worked through the years. We are making our own history. As our retirement nears, we need to take steps to make the transition to new service projects easier. Christians don't retire—they just get promoted to more service.

Spotlight Feature

Cheryl Rogers

In many ways, Cheryl Rogers's work life has gone exactly as planned. When her four children were young, she stayed home and poured herself into their lives. Eventually, they went off to school, and she began her first job outside the home. Although she enjoyed working in a busy procurement office, she found the mission of the large manufacturing company uncompelling. So, she accepted a job change to become territory manager for an in-home comfort care firm. Her duties included scheduling and managing non-medical aides who provided services for (mostly) elderly people in their homes.

Over time, Cheryl found the distance between herself and the services she provided left her wishing for a different kind of job. This evolution is typical of many Christians who continue to grow and learn about their giftings. Although effective at her job, she wanted to impact customers directly.

The next logical leap for Cheryl was to accept a position as an office manager in a doctor's office. Although motherhood remained her primary concern, the hours and demands of her position at the doctor's office fit well into her family's schedule. Almost immediately, she knew this job represented a sweet spot where she could serve Jesus and others effectively. For many years, she continued working in this field and felt fulfilled by the contributions she made.

Cheryl might have been content staying in that environment until retirement, but God had other plans. The office politics turned south, and Cheryl unexpectedly found herself job hunting again. It became a watershed moment in her work life.

Cheryl went through the rigors of job hunting and found a position with an addiction treatment facility near Cincinnati, Ohio. While her first job with the company included plenty of human contact with patients, their families, and other staff members, she soon received a promotion. The move into addiction treatment management was not Cheryl's first choice, but it became obvious the position fit her perfectly. "Part of the job is still to work with patients," she says. "It is so rewarding to hear them talk about getting clean and sober. Their lives totally change. Some weren't even able to be around their families due to their addictions. Now they can spend the holidays with relatives again. They are so grateful for life's blessings."

Cheryl works closely with her staff on human resources matters but still finds herself in close contact with patients and their families. God is welcome at this facility, and Cheryl finds enough room there to share her faith when appropriate. Over time, her ability to care for others has become an obvious part of her skillset. Although she is still ten years or so away from retirement age, she intends to continue serving others as long as she is able. "There are many opportunities at my church that I hope to have more time to participate in," Cheryl says. "My goal is to stay healthy and continue doing what I can until Jesus comes."

Spotlight Questions

What could you identify with in Cheryl's story?

What action steps occurred to you about taking God to work?

Study Questions

1   *Read Psalm 58:11.* What did you hope to get from this study?

2   What is the promise of this verse?

3   Think of a practical definition of righteousness. How can you obtain it? (Hint: the cross of Jesus is involved.)

4   *Read Matthew 6:6.* Why is personal prayer time important?

5   When do you pray?

6   What tools do you use to remember prayer concerns?

7   *Read Matthew 10:38–41.* In what ways are Christians asked to take up their cross?

8   Do you recognize situations where God has asked you to lay down your life for His purposes? Give an example or two.

9   What does it mean to receive a righteous man in the name of a righteous man (see verse 41)?

10 *Read 2 John 1:8.* What does it mean to "look to yourselves, that we don't lose those things we've worked for?"

11 What can you do to ensure you receive a full reward in heaven?

12 *Read Colossians 3:23.* What will you do heartily, as to the LORD and not to men?

Prayer

Thank You, gracious heavenly Father, for Your purpose and plan for my life. Thank You for the vocation to which You have called me and Your help in finding the right situation where I can use my gifts. Open my eyes to the ministry opportunities around me and to those lost and broken ones whom You place in my path. Equip me with Your love, Your wisdom, and Your freedom for the journey. Make me fruitful for Your kingdom and teach me to take care of Your world through my work. At the end of my earthly life, may I be worthy of Your praise for the stewardship of the gifts, talents, finances, and relationships that You have entrusted to me. In the name of Jesus, amen.

What will you do to take God to work this week?

Epilogue

On a clear day in Washington in September 2011, my office at the Department of Homeland Security Office of Procurement Operations buzzed along busily as usual. Employees popped in and out as I tried to prepare for a meeting later in the day. Then, in a moment, everything changed. The whole building began to shake. I got up from my chair and walked into the hallway. The employee in the next office, a diminutive lady, became quite animated.

"Dave," Misha asked, "what's happening?"

"It feels like it might be an earthquake," I said without much conviction. My mind went first to terrorist attack or perhaps a nuclear bomb aimed at the Capitol or White House, both just blocks away.

"I don't want to be alone," Misha said.

"Come in my office," I responded. "You can get under the credenza, and I will get under the desk in case something falls from the ceiling."

As we crawled into cubby holes in the office furniture, I spoke a simple prayer that God would protect us and help us find out what happened. A new set of shakes and rattles began. After a minute or so, the rumbling stopped. The electricity in our building went off, including all but the emergency lights. The windows produced enough light for us to see that we were unharmed and that the office remained intact.

After a minute or two, we emerged from our hiding places and checked on the other people in our group. I used the combination to the secure room and opened the door. With no windows, the employees there had been plunged into complete darkness. Soon, they all made their way into the hallway. Without any other ideas, we filed down the staircase. Some people remained scared and wanted to hurry down. Others encouraged everyone to remain calm.

On that day, I felt glad that I brought God to work. In times of uncertainty, those around us need our faith, and we must be prepared for anything. Beyond just living to be a witness for Christ, people need our help in difficult times. Although these contributions to our colleagues and customers may seem minor at times, our entire presence turns into a reflection of a much greater light: Jesus. Our work life, like the other parts of our lives, isn't really about us. It's all about God and our ability to illuminate a path to Him. "So then neither he who plants is anything, nor he who waters, but God who gives the increase" (1 Corinthians 3:7).

Prayer

Dear Father, only You know the full potential You placed into my life. Show me how to work as unto You. Teach me patience, selfless love for my co-workers, respect for my supervisors, and freedom from low expectations. Show me how to embody superior customer service, beginning with You and extending to all those who depend on the goods and services I provide. Grant me wisdom in every aspect of my job or profession. Let me become a witness that pleases You. In the name of Jesus, amen.

Notes

1. "Religious Discrimination," U.S. Equal Employment Opportunity Commission, https://www.eeoc.gov/laws/types/religion.cfm as noted on February 21, 2018.

2. "More Than Half of U.S. Workers Are Satisfied with Their Jobs," The Conference Board, September 1, 2017, https://www.conference-board.org/press/pressdetail.cfm?pressid=7184, as noted on February 21, 2018.

3. "Living Paycheck to Paycheck Is a Way of Life for Majority of U.S. Workers, According to New CareerBuilder Survey," *Career-Builder*, August 27, 2017, http://press.careerbuilder.com/2017-08-24-Living-Paycheck-to-Paycheck-is-a-Way-of-Life-for-Majority-of-U-S-Workers-According-to-New-CareerBuilder-Survey.

4. "Stress Is Killing You," The American Institute of Stress, www.stress.org/stress-is-killing-you/, as noted on January 18, 2018.

5. "Stress and Your Health," U.S. Department of Health and Human Services, www.womenshealth.gov/a-z-topics/stress-and-your-health, as noted January 18, 2018.

6. "Women: Work, Home, Multiple Roles, and Stress," Cleveland Clinic, https://my.clevelandclinic.org/health/articles/5545-women-work-home-multiple-roles-stress.

7. "'It's on Fire!' Tinker Remembers Bldg. 3001 Inferno of 1984," *Tinker Take Off*, November 12–18, 2004, vol. 62, issue. 45, http://journalrecord.com/tinkertakeoff/category/2004-nov-12-nov-18-vol-62-iss-45/.

Acknowledgements

Pastor Steve Reynolds and David L. Winters would like to acknowledge the substantial support, assistance and friendship provided by the following:

Debbie Reynolds
Susan Fouty
Elizabeth Brown
Gary Hall
Kyle Hansen
Norah Harmon
Nirvana Blatchford-Rodriguez

Andrew Margrave
Byron McKinnon
Mabinty Quarshie
James Raeford
Latonya Stewart
Ana Sufitchi
Danielle Brow

Both authors owe a debt of gratitude to their parents for leading by example in demonstrating a strong work ethic. Thank you Alfred and Betsy Reynolds and Estil and Fern Winters.

Other Titles by Steve Reynolds

Bod 4 God: Twelve Weeks to Lasting Weight Loss
Get Off the Couch: 6 Motivators to Help You Lose Weight and Start Living
The Healthy Renegade Pastor *
Wise Up! *
(* co-authored books)

Other Titles by David L. Winters

Sabbatical of the Mind: The Journey from Anxiety to Peace
Driver Confessional

Made in the USA
Columbia, SC
11 March 2020